STUDIES IN ENGLISH LITERA

Gene

David

D1205101

Already published in the series:

Already published in the series (*continued*):

GERARD MANLEY HOPKINS: THE POEMS

by
R. K. R. THORNTON
Lecturer in English, University of Newcastle upon Tyne

EDWARD ARNOLD

© R. K. R. THORNTON, 1973

First published 1973
by Edward Arnold (Publishers) Ltd,
41 Bedford Square, London WC1B 3DQ

Reprinted 1977, 1979

ISBN: 0 7131 5727 5

Printed and bound in Great Britain at
The Camelot Press Ltd, Southampton

General Preface

The object of this series is to provide studies of individual novels, plays and groups of poems and essays which are known to be widely read by students. The emphasis is on clarification and evaluation; biographical and historical facts, while they may be discussed when they throw light on particular elements in a writer's work, are generally subordinated to critical discussion. What kind of work is this? What exactly goes on here? How good is this work, and why? These are the questions that each writer will try to answer.

It should be emphasized that these studies are written on the assumption that the reader has already read carefully the work discussed. The objective is not to enable students to deliver opinions about works they have not read, nor is it to provide ready-made ideas to be applied to works that have been read. In one sense all critical interpretation can be regarded as foisting opinions on readers, but to accept this is to deny the advantages of any sort of critical discussion directed at students or indeed at anybody else. The aim of these studies is to provide what Coleridge called in another context 'aids to reflection' about the works discussed. The interpretations are offered as suggestive rather than as definitive, in the hope of stimulating the reader into developing further his own insights. This is after all the function of all critical discourse among sensible people.

Because of the interest which this kind of study has aroused, it has been decided to extend it first from merely English literature to include also some selected works of American literature and now further to include selected works in English by Commonwealth writers. The criterion will remain that the book studied is important in itself and is widely read by students.

DAVID DAICHES

Contents

Acknowledgements

The Publishers' thanks are due to the Oxford University Press, by arrangement with the Society of Jesus, for permission to reproduce copyright material from the following works: *The Poems of Gerard Manley Hopkins*, 4th edition, ed. W. H. Gardner and N. H. MacKenzie; *The Journals and Papers of Gerard Manley Hopkins*, ed. Humphry House and Graham Storey; *The Letters of Gerard Manley Hopkins to Robert Bridges*, ed. Claude Colleer Abbott; *The Correspondence of Gerard Manley Hopkins and Richard Watson Dixon*, ed. Claude Colleer Abbott; *Further Letters of Gerard Manley Hopkins*, ed. Claude Colleer Abbott; and *The Sermons and Devotional Writings of Gerard Manley Hopkins*, ed. Christopher Devlin, S.J.

Introduction, Abbreviations, and Bibliography

The intention of this study is always to turn the reader back towards Hopkins's poetry, and to his other writings which support it and have much interest of their own; and the reader will need to have by him a text of the poetry to make proper use of it. Hopkins is, if not always his best critic, certainly his best commentator, and I have therefore used, and urge the reader to get to know, the following books, which I refer to throughout the text under their abbreviated titles:[1]

Poems: *The Poems of Gerard Manley Hopkins*, 4th edn., ed. W. H. Gardner and N. H. MacKenzie (1967).

Letters: *The Letters of Gerard Manley Hopkins to Robert Bridges*, ed. Claude Colleer Abbott (1935, revised 1955).

Correspondence: *The Correspondence of Gerard Manley Hopkins and Richard Watson Dixon*, ed. C. C. Abbott (1935, revised 1955).

Further Letters: *Further Letters of Gerard Manley Hopkins*, 2nd edn., ed. C. C. Abbott (1956).

Journals and Papers: *The Journals and Papers of Gerard Manley Hopkins*, ed. Humphry House and Graham Storey (1959).

Sermons: *The Sermons and Devotional Writings of Gerard Manley Hopkins*, ed. Christopher Devlin, S.J. (1959).

What Hopkins said of one of his unfinished projects, 'a sort of popular account of Light and the Ether', will serve for introduction:

Popular is not quite the word; it is not meant to be easy reading, for such a difficult subject can only be made easy by a very summary and sketchy treatment; rather it is meant for the lay or unprofessional student who will read carefully so long as there are no mathematics and all technicalities are explained; and my hope is to explain things thoroughly and make the matter to such a reader, as far as I go in it, perfectly intelligible.   (*Correspondence*, p. 139)

[1] All the editions listed here are published by the Oxford University Press.

1. Preparation for Poetry: The Background of Ideas

> He is an absolute and unembarrassed instance of a poet, or if we may put it in another way that he is a workman come from his apprenticeship with the Muses skilled to perfection in his trade and having made himself master of all that the science has to give him.
>
> (Hopkins of Richard Garnett, *Journals and Papers*, p. 112)

Hopkins's mastery of his trade made him one of the most distinctive poets in English. Whether his mood is one of delighted affirmation or of dark struggling against despair, his style is unmistakable. While some editors have placed Hopkins at the beginning of their anthologies of modern poetry and some critics have agreed that he is remarkably modern, others have equally correctly insisted that he is solidly Victorian; all agree, as a glance at the poetry will confirm, that the poetry is distinctive. Take any of his poems; *Hurrahing in Harvest* for example:

> Summer ends now; now, barbarous in beauty, the stooks rise
> Around; up above, what wind-walks! what lovely behaviour
> Of silk-sack clouds! has wilder, wilful-wavier
> Meal-drift moulded ever and melted across skies?
>
> I walk, I lift up, I lift up heart, eyes,
> Down all that glory in the heavens to glean our Saviour;
> And, éyes, heárt, what looks, what lips yet gave you a
> Rapturous love's greeting of realer, of rounder replies?
>
> (*Poems*, p. 70)

One immediately notes the exuberant intelligence, the disregard for conventional rhythm, the curious rhyme, the delight in the surface of language, the exploration for the exact nature of both the detail and the word to fit it, and the meticulous difficulty of the interrelationship of the parts. Or take the poem which begins:

> I wake and feel the fell of dark, not day.
> What hours, O what black hoürs we have spent

This night! what sights you, heart, saw; ways you went!
And more must, in yet longer light's delay.

With witness I speak this. But where I say
Hours I mean years, mean life. And my lament
Is cries countless, cries like dead letters sent
To dearest him that lives alas! away.

(*Poems*, p. 101)

The passionate commitment of this poem, strengthened rather than weakened by its struggle within a tight form and a complex syntax, seems continually fresh. In 1918, when the first edition of Hopkins's poems was published, they seemed at the same time startlingly new and curiously in keeping with the mood and style of the new century. It was as if Hopkins had single-handed and almost in private pushed English poetry thirty years beyond the Victorian period to which he belonged.

It was nonetheless something of an accident that they should appear so late, illustrating what Hopkins said of the tardiness of fame in his first letter to a neglected poet who became an important correspondent and friend, R. W. Dixon: 'Many beautiful works have been almost unknown and then have gained fame at last'. Hopkins died in 1889, and during his life allowed very little, and none of the most distinctive, of his work to be published. His poetic fame rested in the hands of Robert Bridges, his friend, his other major correspondent, a fellow poet and later Poet Laureate. Although Bridges quickly planned an edition of Hopkins's work, and did indeed publish a small number of poems and fragments in the intervening years (without much response from the critics), it was not until 1918 that the bulk of his poetry was generally available, and it was another ten years before it achieved any degree of popularity. Only then had critical opinion caught up with the ideas and practices doggedly developed from solidly nineteenth-century bases by a man who sought in all things for extremes of perfection.

He was born in 1844 into an artistic family. His father had published a book of poems in the previous year, and two of his brothers were to become professional artists. In his Grammar School days at Highgate he revealed a surprisingly rigorous notion of self-discipline, a love of poetry, and a keen intelligence. The first resulted in smaller feats of self-control like his abstaining from all liquids for a week in order to win a bet, and in the larger and more general habit of mind which was to accept readily the rigidity of Jesuit discipline and apply it too rigorously, to himself in particular; the second was the start of that lifelong passion for poetry which was often in conflict with his asceticism; and the third won him an exhibition to Balliol College, Oxford. It was at Oxford that Hopkins became a Roman Catholic, and, after taking a First in 'Classics' in 1867, he taught and thought for a while before deciding to become a priest in 1868.

He entered the Jesuit novitiate and studied at Roehampton until 1870 and then at Stonyhurst until 1873. After a year's teaching back at Roehampton, he studied theology at St Bueno's College, St Asaph, between 1874 and 1877 before being ordained priest in September 1877. His superiors tried him at a variety of jobs in his years as a priest: select preacher at Farm Street in London, for a short time in Leigh in Lancashire, for a longer spell at St Francis Xavier's Church in Liverpool, and again for a short time in Glasgow. In 1881 he went back to Roehampton for his third year of noviceship before taking his last vows. From 1882 he was employed mainly as a teacher and—a job which he found particularly irksome—as examiner, first at Stonyhurst College, and finally as Professor of Greek at University College, Dublin, and Fellow of the Royal University of Ireland. He died of typhoid fever on 8 June 1889.

The central point to note about this brief biographical sketch is Hopkins's commitment to religion before literature, a commitment which he himself frequently emphasized. Where he did take time to consider literature, it was usually because he was teaching it rather than writing, as one can see from his final years as Professor of Greek or from his earlier years at Roehampton, from which period his lecture notes on *Rhythm and the other structural parts of Rhetoric—verse* and on *Poetry and verse* survive. Hopkins wished to sacrifice his life to the service of God; and if he wished to dedicate his life to God, he also wished every part of it, not excluding his poetry, to be dedicated to the same end. Poetry often seemed to him a luxury for which he could not always afford time away from what he thought of as his proper duties, but it was never disconnected from his religious ideas:

> I cannot in conscience spend time on poetry, neither have I the inducements and inspirations that make others compose. Feeling, love in particular, is the great moving power and spring of verse and the only person that I am in love with seldom, especially now, stirs my heart sensibly and when he does I cannot always 'make capital' of it, it would be a sacrilege to do so. Then again I have of myself made verse so laborious.   (*Letters*, p. 66)

If his life as a priest determined to a large extent the aim of his poetry, it had an important effect on its nature also by isolating him from a great deal of contemporary literature and from public criticism. His usual companions were not poets or even critics, and he did not have or allow himself a great deal of time to keep up with developments in literature. He developed his own methods and ideas and in doing so went further than and often in different directions from contemporary writers, partly because he was forced back on his own initiatives and partly as a result of having no Victorian general audience to please. Instead he had as his main and almost his only audience two careful, committed and friendly poets, willing to exchange views and to listen thoughtfully and with interest to his astonishing ideas and the remarkable poetry which resulted. In a letter to Bridges (*Letters*, p. 196) Hopkins listed his small audience of about a dozen or so, and he was always unwilling to strive to increase that number or to publish his poems. He claimed that it was up to God to choose whether to make them better known: 'if he chooses to avail himself of what I leave at his disposal he can do so with a felicity and with a success which I could never command' (*Correspondence*, p. 93).

This isolation from the main current of literature, except for contact with writers themselves concerned with questions of style, metre and language, meant that Hopkins followed the logic of the idea rather than the current fashion. Even in his letters on matters of technique and interpretation, it seems that with Dixon Hopkins is the teacher rather than the pupil, and with Bridges it is a matter of discussion without either being completely convinced by the other. Taking his logic to great lengths, Hopkins created a poetry vastly different from that of his contemporaries, though his point of departure is firmly in his time.

Hopkins is one of the most logical of poets. Though his themes and his treatment often seem to derive from emotion and have an effect on the emotions, they grow from more single-minded thinking about the nature of poetry and its technical and philosophical implications before putting pen to paper than is the case with any other English poet. He was himself aware of his love of—or rather his natural inability to avoid —logicality. In a letter to R. W. Dixon he remarked of the latter's poem *Fallen Rain* that 'a perverse over-perspectiveness of mind nudges me that the rain could never be wooed by the rainbow which only comes into being by its falling nor could witness the wooing when made any more than the quicksilver can look from the out side back into the glass'. Two years later he remembered the occasion: 'You must have been shocked at my objection from perspective. But thoughts of that sort haunt me' (*Correspondence*, pp. 20 and 48). An understanding of the fundamental logicality of Hopkins's mind is essential if we are to grasp the nature of his poetry and see how to get to its methods and meanings when these are obscure.

It was another of those shapely accidents which gave Hopkins the time to consider his theories. He had written poetry in his youth, and indeed intended to make a career of either art or literature. But when he joined the Society of Jesus in 1868, he gave up that ambition for what he felt was a more important one. He explained to R. W. Dixon that, after the 'slaughter of the innocents'—his rather rueful reference to the burning of his manuscripts—he stopped composing poetry:

> You ask, do I write verse myself. What I had written I burnt before I became a Jesuit and resolved to write no more, as not belonging to my profession, unless it were by the wish of my superiors; so for seven years I wrote nothing but two or three little presentation pieces which occasion called for.   (*Correspondence*, p. 14)

If he gave up the writing of poetry, he did not give up the things which were the constituent parts of his poetry: the subject matter, the purpose, and the techniques of both language and versification. Those seven years, and indeed longer, for he had abstained from poetry at times before then, were spent in both private and professional exploration of material and ways of thinking which laid a carefully-considered system of ideas behind the eventual outburst of seemingly spontaneous poetry. In the last sonnet sent to Robert Bridges, a poem about loss of inspiration written only two months before his death, he refers to the length of time spent in considering his poems. First comes inspiration:

> The fine delight that fathers thought; the strong
> Spur, live and lancing like the blowpipe flame,
> Breathes once and, quenchèd faster than it came,
> Leaves yet the mind a mother of immortal song.

Then comes the lengthy consideration:

> Nine months she then, nay years, nine years she long
> Within her wears, bears, cares and combs the same:
> The widow of an insight lost she lives, with aim
> Now known and hand at work now never wrong.
>
> (*Poems*, p. 108)

We can trace much of the process in the records he left in undergraduate essays, notes for lectures, private notes, journals and other papers; and the many years spent considering his craft go a long way to explaining the superficial complexity and the fundamental coherence of his work. He was drifting quite steadily towards that splendid cataract of poetry of the years from 1876 to 1889, and a glance at the years before 1876 will serve to indicate that the poems are the natural outcome of the poet's life and thought, and not separate from his other occupations.

He was always interested in language, and his earliest surviving diary includes a large number of notes on language and the connection and derivation of words, probably because the examination for which he was preparing at the time required information of that sort. Hopkins's interest went beyond the mere necessities, and the effect went beyond the examination; he did get a First in Moderations (the first part of his Classics degree), but his poetry of over eleven years later still carries the marks of a man interested in the connections between meanings and sounds and the interrelationship of words. Take this from his diary of 1863:

> Grind, gride, gird, grit, groat, grate, greet, κρούειν, crush, crash, κροτεῖν, etc.
> Original meaning to *strike*, *rub*, particularly *together*, That which is produced by such means is the *grit*, the *groats* or crumbs, like *fragmentum* from *frangere*, *bit* from *bite*. *Crumb*, *crumble* perhaps akin. To *greet*, to strike the hands together (?). *Greet*, grief, wearing, *tribulation*. *Grief* possibly connected. *Gruff*, with a sound as of two things rubbing together. I believe these words to be onomatopoetic. *Gr* common to them all representing a particular sound. In fact I think the onomatopoetic theory has not had a fair chance. Cf. *Crack, creak, croak, crake, graculus, crackle*. These must be onomatopoetic.
>
> (*Journals and Papers*, p. 5)

In the poetry of his later years words from this group occur several times when Hopkins writes of a painful trial, a moment when some force (usually either directly or indirectly from God) brings a man to an extreme and separates the chaff from the grain. In *The Wreck of the Deutschland* Paul is said to be converted 'at a crash', just as Hopkins is converted in another sense 'at a trumpet crash', in *That Nature is a Heraclitean Fire*; in *God's Grandeur* the effect is 'like the ooze of oil/ Crushed'; in *Spelt from Sibyl's Leaves* 'thoughts against thoughts in groans grind'. A whole group of Hopkins's central notions, of punishment, sorrow, self-abrading thought, recognition of God in moments of stress, harvest and the releasing of essences, is thus seen by Hopkins as related even in the nature of the language. At other times, where he is clear that there is no historical or semantic connection of words, he is able to force them into connection by emphasizing their similarities of sound, and making a point of their similarities or differences of sense.

His interest in language was not simply in vocabulary; it was also in dialect and syntax, in fact in anything curious or distinctive about usage. 'Br. Coupe calls a basket a *whisket*' he noted on 22 February 1869; on 30 April he noted:

> Br. Wells calls a grindstone a *grindlestone*.
> To *lead* north-country for to *carry* (a field of hay etc). *Geet* north-country preterite of *get*: 'he geet agate agoing'.
> Trees sold 'top and lop': Br. Rickaby told me and suggests *top* is the higher, outer, and lighter wood good for firing only, *lop* the stem and bigger boughs when the rest has been lopped off used for timber.
> (*Journals and Papers*, p. 191)

In January of 1868 he noted down what his three-and-a-half-year-old cousin said, obviously delighted by the childish logic which made intelligible sense by creating new combinations on analogy with existing usage: 'Being mimicked by Mabel she cried "Sissie not mock Baby! Baby good mind to cut Sissie."—*Did be to go* = was going to go—*Baby-cuts* = little scissors—*Church-pockie* = alms'-box'(*Journals and Papers*, p. 160). Thus, all the time that Hopkins was not writing poetry, he was nonetheless concerned with the way that people speak, the sounds and the meanings of words, and the way in which the language worked at a fundamental level.

A second of his basic interests, one which was forwarded by his occupation, was in the form of poetry, a subject on which he had to lecture; and his lecture notes tell us a good deal about how his ideas were developing. As Graham Storey wrote in the Preface to *Journals and Papers*, 'It is important to realize that the stimulus to formulate his thoughts about metre came directly from the teaching he was officially given to do', while at Roehampton (p. xxvii). As usual Hopkins started from basic principles, and based his notions on a wide range of examples, from Hebrew, Greek, Latin, Icelandic, Middle English, Spanish, Welsh, French and Italian. The lecture notes are admirably clear expositions of some of the characteristics of verse, the nature of rhythm, the nature of rhyme, alliteration, assonance, and their use in different times and countries; but two things stand out, his notion of rhythm and his notion of the nature of poetry.

It was in analysing and explaining poetic rhythm that he hit upon what seemed to him a new rhythm. He called the common rhythm of English verse Running Rhythm; that is, a rhythm marked off in regular repetitions of a rigid basic unit. So, if the unit is an iambic foot (an unstressed syllable followed by a stressed syllable and written x '), the basic rhythm is iambic:

> x ｜ x ｜ x ｜ x ｜
> I walk my breezy belvedere
>   x ｜   x ｜ x ｜x ｜
> To watch the low or levant sun.

> (*Poems*, p. 25)

If the unit is an anapaestic foot (two unstressed syllables followed by a stressed syllable, x x '), the rhythm is anapaestic:

> x x ｜ x x   ｜ x x ｜ x   x ｜
> It was made of earth's mould but it went from men's eyes
> x x ｜ x x ｜ x x ｜ x   x ｜
> And its place is a secret and shut in the skies.

> (*Poems*, p. 38)

These two rhythms, and rhythms made from repeating the trochee (' x) or the dactyl (' x x), are the commonest measures in English poetry. It is quite obvious that repetition of this sort would eventually become tedious, and so the common practice of poets before the advent of much freer verse systems in the late nineteenth century, and still in metrically more traditional poetry, has been to add interest to the pattern by variation from the basic unit, by reversing it, by omitting one of the syllables, or by some other change. In Hopkins's *The Habit of Perfection*, the first word of the fifth stanza reverses the normal iambic pattern:

> ｜ x   x ｜ x ｜ x ｜
> Nostrils, your careless breath that spend
> x ｜ x ｜ x   ｜ x ｜
> Upon the stir and keep of pride.

> (*Poems*, p. 32)

When this variation from the basic pattern happened in more than one foot of otherwise Running Rhythm, Hopkins said that we have Counterpoint Rhythm. This means that we keep the idea of the basic rhythm in our heads and hear on top of it the actual rhythm of the line. So in

Paradise Regained, to use Hopkins's example, the basic rhythm is iambic but the actual rhythm is very different and we are aware of both:

```
Basic rhythm    x  ' x  '   x  '    x ' x '
Actual rhythm    '   x x  '   x  '    ' x  x '
```
            Home to his mother's house private returned.

In order to be able to appreciate Counterpoint Rhythm, one must have a Running Rhythm established; if a poem were entirely counterpointed there would be no way of establishing the basic rhythm, and one would be approaching the new metre which Hopkins was developing, a metre which was both radically different from Victorian metrical practice and allowed much more variety while being basically very simple. Torn as so often between his love of rules and his love of freedom, Hopkins cited precedents in Classical verse, English children's rhymes, weather saws, and Middle English verse. The simple change was to make the unit to be repeated no longer rigid; it must have one stressed syllable, but this could be followed by anything from none to three (and in special cases more) unstressed syllables. The result of this theory of versification is that Hopkins felt free to write lines that at one extreme have the filigree lightness of this line from stanza 31 of *The Wreck of the Deutschland*:

```
 '  x  x x '  x  x  x x x '   x x  ' x x x   x   '   x  x
```
            Finger of a tender of, O of a feathery delicacy, the breast of the

where there are only five stresses (and therefore five feet) in twenty-one syllables, and at the other extreme have the ominous strength of this line from stanza 11:

```
     x '   '    '    x   x '   '    '    '
```
            The sour scythe cringe, and the blear share come,

where there are six stresses (and therefore six feet) in nine syllables. The rhythm as so far described would be very similar to prose rhythm, but it is distinguished by considering the feet as having an equality of strength or length or time, as in musical bars. One of the features of the rhythm is that one stress can follow immediately after another, sprung sharply like a trap or a surprise. This seems to be the reason that Hopkins called it Sprung Rhythm, writing to Dixon that

I should add that the word Sprung which I use for this rhythm means something like *abrupt* and applies by rights only where one stress follows another running, without syllable between. Besides the bare principle which I have been explaining I employ various artifices which you will see in reading. (*Correspondence*, p. 23)

His lecture notes show that most of the theory of Sprung Rhythm was ready in his mind before he began writing his poetry.

A third element in his long preparation for poetry was his 'free long looking' at the world around him. At times he denied himself even that; in a Journal entry for 24 January 1869, he recorded that 'a penance which I was doing from Jan. 25 to July 25 prevented my seeing much that half-year' (*Journals and Papers*, p. 190). More usually he recorded in his Journal the results of his unique combination of talents, the analytical power of a scientist, the shaping eye of an artist, and the power of expression of a poet. Sometimes one can merely admire the potentialities for poetry in the passages:

> The mountains and in particular the Silberhorn are shaped and nippled like the sand in an hourglass and the Silberhorn has a subsidiary pyramidal peak naped sharply down the sides. Then one of their beauties is in nearly vertical places the fine pleatings of the snow running to or from one another, like the newness of lawn in an alb and sometimes cut off short as crisp as celery.
>
> There are round one of the heights of the Jungfrau two ends or falls of a glacier. If you took the skin of a white tiger or the deep fell of some other animal and swung it tossing high in the air and then cast it out before you it would fall and so clasp and lap round anything in its way just as this glacier does and the fleece would part in the same rifts: you must suppose a lazuli under-flix to appear. The spraying out of one end I tried to catch but it would have taken hours: it was this which first made me think of a tiger-skin, and it ends in tongues and points like the tail and claws: indeed the ends of the glaciers are knotted or knuckled like talons. (*Journals and Papers*, p. 174)

That is from 1868, but bears the same stamp as this from five years later:

> Water high at Hodder Roughs; where lit from within looking like pale gold, elsewhere velvety brown like ginger syrop; heavy locks or brushes like shaggy rope-ends rolling from a corner of the falls and one huddling over another; below the rock the bubble-jestled skirt of foam jumping back against the fall, which cuts its way clean and will not let it through, and there spitting up in long white ragged shots and bushes like a mess of thongs of bramble, and I saw by looking over nearer that those looping watersprigs that lace and dance and jockey in the air are strung of single drops, the end one, like a tassel or a heavier bead, the biggest; they look like bubbles in a quill. When

the air caught at the sill of the fall a sour yellow light flushed under-
neath like smoke kindling all along the rock, with a sullen noise which
we thought was thunder till someone pointed out the cause, and this
happened, I noticed, when one of the bladders or blisters that form
and come bumping to the top in troubled water sailed over the falls.
(*Journals and Papers*, p. 233)

Sometimes the relationship between the Journals and the poems is
evident, and helpful in understanding them. *Spelt from Sibyl's Leaves*
obviously recalls the experience of almost fifteen years earlier when
Hopkins first saw the Northern Lights, and some of the details of the
poem and its overall design are suggested and clarified in this passage:

My eye was caught by beams of light and dark very like the crown of
horny rays the sun makes behind a cloud. At first I thought of silvery
cloud until I saw that these were more luminous and did not dim the
clearness of the stars in the Bear. They rose slightly radiating thrown
out from the earthline. Then I saw soft pulses of light one after another
rise and pass upwards arched in shape but waveringly and with the
arch broken. They seemed to float, not following the warp of the
sphere as falling stars look to do but free though concentrical with it.
This busy working of nature wholly independent of the earth and
seeming to go on in a strain of time not reckoned by our reckoning of
days and years but simpler and as if correcting the preoccupation of
the world by being preoccupied with and appealing to and dated to
the day of judgment was like a new witness to God and filled me with
delightful fear.   (*Journals and Papers*, p. 200)

The light and dark, the horny rays, the strain of time, and the reminder
of judgment day 'correcting the preoccupation of the world' support
interpretations of the later poem. Sometimes merely a detail used in the
poetry flashes from the Journal, the 'Chestnuts as bright as coals or spots
of vermilion' (p. 189) of 1868 coming transformed into *Pied Beauty* as
'Fresh-firecoal chestnut-falls' nine years later. Sometimes the Journal
merely indicates that he was keeping his poet's eye in.

The observations in his Journal became less and less random as he
developed his search for laws, for the rule or the pattern in the thing he
was observing, what made it what it was. As he expressed it later in a
letter to Bridges, 'as air, melody, is what strikes me most of all in music
and design in painting, so design, pattern or what I am in the habit of
calling "inscape" is what I above all aim at in poetry. Now it is the virtue

of design, pattern, or inscape to be distinctive and it is the vice of distinctiveness to become queer' (*Letters*, p. 66). There are numerous examples of his search for the laws of things, and he tried various words for this law or pattern. In June 1866 he

> Was happily able to see composition of the crowd in the area of the theatre, all the heads looking one way thrown up by their black coats relieved only by white shirt-fronts etc: the short strokes of eyes, nose, mouth, repeated hundreds of times I believe it is which gives the visible law: looked at in any one instance it flies. I could find a sort of beauty in this, certainly character—but in fact that is almost synonymous with finding order, anywhere.　　(*Journals and Papers*, p. 139)

In July he looked at oaks and found 'the organisation of this tree is difficult' (p. 144). Later in the same month, two days after recording another perception that 'I saw clearly the impossibility of staying in the Church of England', he noted that 'I have now found the law of the oak leaves' (p. 146). He was searching for some unifying principle. In 1872 he saw it in the sea: 'In watching the sea one should be alive to the oneness which all its motion and tumult receives from its perpetual balance and falling this way and that to its level' (p. 225). In 1867 he saw it in a landscape:

> When I got to the middle of the common they call Knighton Heathfields (for heaths they call heathfields here) I saw the wholeness of the sky and the sun like its ace.　　(p. 154)

He soon developed a word for describing the pattern of a thing, the way it is made, its 'make' as he sometimes called it; and he made up his word on analogy with words like 'landscape'. If the picture that makes a whole and single thing out of an area of land is a landscape, then what makes up a single thing out of its inner nature would be its 'inscape'. And the word occurs frequently in his descriptions of the world about him as he observes distinctive natures and tries to define them in words. In 1874 he went to get an impression of a sham fight, but was too early:

> however got this—caught that inscape in the horse that you see in the pediment especially and other basreliefs of the Parthenon and even which Sophocles had felt and expresses in two choruses of the *Oedipus Coloneus*, running on the likeness of a horse to a breaker, a wave of the sea curling over. I looked at the groin or the flank and saw how the set of the hair symmetrically flowed outwards from it to all parts of

the body, so that, following that one may inscape the whole beast very simply.   (pp. 241–2)

In that passage one can also see Hopkins's willingness to develop words, the noun 'inscape' giving rise to a verb 'to inscape' which means roughly 'to grasp the pattern of' or sometimes 'to show the pattern of'.

The description of the inner nature of something in words which try to capture its distinctiveness was not enough. In a famous passage about the bluebell, Hopkins shows how he was beginning to think of the inscape of natural things not just as the principle of their organization but also as the implication of an organizing power behind them and the expression of the nature of God in them:

> I do not think I have ever seen anything more beautiful than the blue-bell I have been looking at. I know the beauty of our Lord by it. Its inscape is mixed of strength and grace, like an ash tree.   (p. 199)

He saw both order and purpose in the patterns:

> All the world is full of inscape and chance left free to act falls into an order as well as purpose: looking out of my window I caught it in the random clods and broken heaps of snow made by the cast of a broom. The same of the path trenched by footsteps in ankledeep snow across the fields leading to Hodder wood through which we went to see the river.   (p. 230)

Hopkins's training as a Jesuit, for him the main occupation of these years, would incline him to see nature in this way. The Principle and Foundation of the Ignatian Exercises, with which Hopkins was more than familiar, sent him in that direction:

> Man was created to praise, reverence and serve God Our Lord, and by so doing to save his soul. And the other things on the face of the earth were created for man's sake and to help him in the carrying out of the end for which he was created.   (*Sermons*, p. 122)

This sort of idea mixed easily with two other sources of thought for Hopkins, one Catholic and one non-Catholic, but both seeing God in nature. Ruskin had not only used the word 'law' to describe the pattern of a thing, but also inclined to the same reading into that law a notion of its creator. In a passage from his autobiographical *Praeterita* (1885–9), Ruskin recalled the early experience at Fontainebleau of a moment of realization that was to shape his subsequent thought, a very Hopkins-like moment. He had decided to draw an aspen:

Languidly, but not idly, I began to draw it; and as I drew, the langour passed away: the beautiful lines insisted on being traced,—without weariness. More and more beautiful they became, as each rose out of the rest, and took its place in the air. With wonder increasing every instant, I saw that they 'composed' themselves, by finer laws than any known of men. At last, the tree was there, and everything that I had thought before about trees, nowhere.

. . . The woods, which I had only looked on as wilderness, fulfilled I then saw, in their beauty, the same laws which guided the clouds, divided the light, and balanced the wave. 'He hath made everything beautiful, in his time,' became for me thenceforward the interpretation of the bond between the human mind and all visible things; and I returned along the wood-road feeling that it had led me far;—Farther than ever fancy had reached, or theodolite measured.

Ruskin had the same penetrating eye to reach out for and grasp the laws of the trees, the clouds, the light, and water, subjects which were also for Hopkins almost an obsession, and he has the same insistence on the link between man and God through nature. Duns Scotus, a thirteenth-century Catholic philosopher of whom I shall say a little more in a later chapter, not only provided Hopkins with some authority in considering it important to value the distinguishing characteristics of things but also suggested a view of the Incarnation which became central to his thinking. In crude terms, while the usual view is that God became man to redeem man's sin and as a consequence of that sin, Hopkins followed Scotus in believing that God willed from eternity to become man as an act of love and whether or not man chose to sin, made the world in consequence and used the Incarnation incidentally to redeem man. So Hopkins 'saw creation as dependent upon the decree of the Incarnation, and not the other way round' (*Sermons*, p. 109). All created things therefore were in a sense aspects of the Incarnation, and could show forth God's purpose. Since he felt that the force which shaped the world and the individualities of its parts was so important, he again coined a word, again by analogy. The pattern of a thing was its inscape, so that the force which made the pattern was its 'instress'. Realizing, as Ruskin did, that the law or inscape had such a profound effect on him, he felt that he needed a word to signify the impact of the perceived pattern on the beholder and, obviously feeling that it was in a sense a continuation of the shaping force, he used the same word, 'instress'. To put it in a way which does not allow for the subtleties and shades of meaning which it acquires for Hopkins, there is a force (instress) which makes natural things the way they are (shapes their inscape) and there is a power (instress) which this shape has to affect the beholder. But as he often pointed out, although these inscapes are everywhere, they have to be looked for and worked for, 'caught'— implying a response—rather than just 'seen':

> I thought how sadly beauty of inscape was unknown and buried away from simple people and yet how near at hand it was if they had eyes to see it and it could be called out everywhere again.
>
> *(Journals and Papers*, p. 221)

There is one more basic essential of Hopkins's poetry to note, perhaps the most fundamental of all, his love of parallel, balance, antithesis, apposition, all modes of comparison which allow things to reveal their particular differences and their fundamental relationships. It was balance that he saw as creating the oneness of the sea, and it is balance that creates the oneness of each of his poems, giving it its own distinctive shape, its law, its inscape, so that it too can partake of the Incarnation and show forth God's purpose. That, at least, was the intention. The tendency towards this point is clear in an essay written for Walter Pater in 1865 on 'The Origin of Our Moral Ideas':

> All thought is of course in a sense an effort an unity [*sic*]. This may be pursued analytically as in science or synthetically as in art or morality. In art it is essential to recognise and strive to realise on a more or less wide basis this unity in some shape or other. It seems also that the desire for unity, for an ideal, is the only definition which will satisfy the historical phenomena of morality. There is an important difference to be noted here. In art we strive to realise not only unity, permanence of law, likeness, but also, with it, difference, variety, contrast: it is rhyme we like, not echo, and not unison but harmony. But in morality the highest consistency is the highest excellence.
>
> *(Journals and Papers*, p. 83)

Even this large antithesis between art and morality is used when Hopkins moves from artistic realization of opposites and variety to a moral realization of unity, as in *Pied Beauty* to take a simple example.

In his Platonic dialogue *On the Origin of Beauty*, a long and intriguing discussion of his ideas, Hopkins has his Professor of Aesthetics expound the theory that beauty can 'be considered as regularity or likeness tempered by irregularity or difference' as a result of which 'All beauty may by a metaphor be called rhyme' (*Journals and Papers*, pp. 101-2).

The parallels to which he is referring here are various: repetitions of grammatical form, whether sentence, clause, phrase or construction; repetition of idea; repetition of pitch; repetition of length of syllable, or stress of syllable; repetition of vowels or consonants, initial or final. The parallelism does not involve sameness, and between the opposites Hopkins was always able to see gradations which added to the beauty of the whole. But it seems that the central nature of poetry for Hopkins is repetition:

> Poetry is speech framed for contemplation of the mind by the way of hearing or speech framed to be heard for its own sake and interest even over and above its interest of meaning. Some matter and meaning is essential to it but only as an element necessary to support and employ the shape which is contemplated for its own sake. (Poetry is in fact speech only employed to carry the inscape of speech for the inscape's sake—and therefore the inscape must be dwelt on. Now if this can be done without repeating it *once* of the inscape will be enough for art and beauty and poetry but then at least the inscape must be understood as so standing by itself that it could be copied and repeated. If not/ repetition, *oftening*, *over-and-overing*, *aftering* of the inscape must take place in order to detach it to the mind and in this light poetry is speech which afters and oftens its inscape, speech couched in a repeating figure and verse is spoken sound having a repeating figure.)
>
> (*Journals and Papers*, p. 289)

In an essay of 1864 *On the Signs of Health and Decay in the Arts* Hopkins wrote of the cause of our sense of the beautiful:

> It is enough to say that it is believed this cause is comparison, the apprehension of the presence of more than one thing, and that it is inseparable in a higher or lower degree from thought. We may perhaps make four degrees or dimensions of it, of which each, as in mathematics, exists and is implied in the dimension above it; these will be those drawn from the comparison (i), of existence with non-existence, of the conception of a thing with the former absence of the conception;—this is an inseparable accident of all thought; (ii), of a thing with itself so as to see in it the continuance of law, in which is implied the comparison of continuance of law with non-continuance; instances of this kind are a straight line or a circle; (iii) of two or more things together, so as to include the principles of Dualism, Plurality, Repetition, Parallelism, and Variety, Contrast, Antithesis; (iv) of finite with infinite things, which can only be done by suggestion; this is the ἀρχή of the Suggestive, the Picturesque and the Sublime.

Art is concerned with the last two of these classes; sometimes with the third, sometimes with both the third and fourth.

(*Journals and Papers*, p. 74)

Many of the difficulties of Hopkins's poetry are quickly resolved by a consciousness of this basic principle of repetition.

Hopkins was the 'master of all that the science has to give him' before a single one of his major poems was written. Much of the work necessary to their composition was done before 1875, but the essential fusion and development into the finished poems was yet to come.

> These things, these things were here and but the beholder
> Wanting; which two when they once meet,
> The heart rears wings bold and bolder
> And hurls for him, O half hurls earth for him off under his feet.

(*Poems*, p. 70)

2. 'The Wreck of the Deutschland'

It is not surprising that the poem which Hopkins wrote after seven or more years of such committed and complex thinking-out of his poetic principles and developing them beyond their superficial implications should be large and complicated. In the event it is the longest and probably the most complex poem he ever wrote, so forbidding that Robert Bridges described it in the notes to his edition of the poems as 'a great dragon folded in the gate to forbid all entrance' and advised the reader 'to circumvent him and attack him later in the rear'. But it is the traditional characteristic of dragons to guard treasure, and this dragon is no exception.

Two things combined to bring Hopkins to the point of breaking his poetic fast, the events of the wreck and the perceptiveness of his rector, who seems to have seen that Hopkins needed to write. Hopkins told Dixon that

> when in the winter of '75 the Deutschland was wrecked in the mouth of the Thames and five Franciscan nuns, exiles from Germany by the Falck Laws, aboard of her were drowned I was affected by the account and happening to say so to my rector he said that he wished someone would write a poem on the subject. On this hint I set to work and, though my hand was out at first, produced one. I had long had

haunting my ear the echo of a new rhythm which now I realised on paper.   (*Correspondence*, p. 14)

He used the opportunity not only to try out his Sprung Rhythm, but also to find expression for many of the other things which were occupying his mind.

The wreck of the ship was in itself sensational. The newspapers were full of it for some days and Hopkins saw several accounts. Some which obviously influenced him even found their way into the fabric and phrasing of the poem. The ship ran aground on a Monday and, as *The Times* reported on 11 December:

> After 3 a.m. on Tuesday morning a scene of horror was witnessed. Some passengers clustered for safety within or upon the wheelhouse, and on the top of other slight structures on deck. Most of the crew and many of the emigrants went into the rigging, where they were safe enough as long as they could maintain their hold. But the intense cold and long exposure told a tale. The purser of the ship, though a strong man, relaxed his grasp, and fell into the sea. Women and children and men were one by one swept away from their shelters on the deck. Five German nuns, whose bodies are now in the dead-house here, clasped hands and were drowned together, the chief sister, a gaunt woman 6 ft. high, calling out loudly and often 'O Christ, come quickly!' till the end came. The shrieks and sobbing of women and children are described by the survivors as agonising. One brave sailor, who was safe in the rigging, went down to try and save a child or woman who was drowning on deck. He was secured by a rope to the rigging, but a wave dashed him against the bulwarks, and when daylight dawned his headless body, detained by the rope, was seen swaying to and fro with the waves. (Quoted in *Further Letters*, pp. 442–3)

It is easy to see the relationship between this account and elements in the central stanzas of the poem. But the wreck was not just a wreck for Hopkins. He told his mother that 'It made a deep impression on me, more than any other wreck or accident I ever read of' (*Further Letters*, p. 135). Alfred Thomas, S.J., in his account of *Hopkins the Jesuit: the Years of Training*[1] says that 'One would like to know why this particular shipwreck should have given rise to the poem' (p. 168). I suggest the answer is that this wreck combined elements which made its effect resonant and deep, and that Hopkins saw in it two central and balancing movements which continually occupied his thoughts: first, God moving

[1] London, 1969.

towards man or showing himself to man; second, man's response to God. Each of these has its own balancing and contrasting sides: God shows himself to man in both the beautiful and the terrifying; man's response may be acceptance, especially saying yes to him at a moment of crisis, recognizing him under great stress, as the nun had done, or it may be refusal of God, his works and his workers. Hopkins emphasized the significance of this last refusal, something hurtful to his pride as a priest, by carefully noting that the nuns were exiles both in his account to Dixon and in the dedication of the poem itself. The poem was to be a new Annunciation, a new assertion of God's place in the world, and Hopkins filled it with examples which parallel those elements he saw in the wreck, with an affirmation of acceptance.

It was clear to him that he was not simply making an account of a shipwreck. He wrote to Bridges, whose friendly if rather grudging criticism has usefully provided us with Hopkins's rejoinders and explanations, that 'The Deutschland would be more generally interesting if there were more wreck and less discourse, I know, but still it is an ode and not primarily a narrative' (*Letters*, p. 49). And he insisted that Bridges, who vowed on first reading that he would never read it again, should not take his first impressions as final:

> Now they say that vessels sailing from the port of London will take (perhaps it should be/used once to take) Thames water for the voyage: it was foul and stunk at first as the ship worked but by degrees casting its filth was in a few days very pure and sweet and wholesomer and better than any water in the world. However that maybe, it is true to my purpose. When a new thing, such as my ventures in the Deutschland are, is presented us our first criticisms are not our truest, best, most homefelt, or most lasting but what come easiest on the instant. They are barbarous and like what the ignorant and the ruck say. This was so with you. The Deutschland on her first run worked very much and unsettled you, thickening and clouding your mind with vulgar mudbottom and common sewage (I see that I am going it with the image) and just then unhappily you *drew off* your criticisms all stinking (a necessity now of the image) and bilgy, whereas if you had let your thoughts cast themselves they would have been clearer in themselves and more to my taste too.   (*Letters*, pp. 50–51)

With this criticism went advice on how to read the poem again: 'pay attention to the best and most intelligible stanzas, as the two last of each part and the narrative of the wreck' (p. 46). One can see the reason for this advice not only in the intelligibility of the stanzas but also in their content, the last two of each part being prayers, with the narrative of the wreck coming between. The two prayers concern man's decision whether or not to acknowledge God, and the wreck is the central and largest example of both the material with which man has to strive and the reaching down of God to man. Thus the two reciprocal movements are central to the stanzas which Hopkins suggested as starting points.

This hints at a fruitful way of looking at a poem which develops and is held together by a series of balances and distinctions. Hopkins moves by a juxtaposition of narratives, events, ideas, words and phrases, in a sort of apposition where things are seen to be different but fundamentally the same. It is a sort of music too, a fugue with repetitions of individual words (John E. Keating in his monograph on the poem[2] lists over 150 words which occur more than once) and on the larger scale repetition of motifs and whole structures. The central idea from which all the others develop is the Incarnation. If one can imagine a border between abstract and concrete, between the transient and the eternal, between the human and the divine, it is this border and the crossing of it that interested and occupied Hopkins; and the Incarnation, God made man, was for him the type of the act of crossing that boundary, and as Scotus had taught him, the source of all creation. The central biblical passage concerning the Incarnation is in St John's gospel where (i. 14) the 'Word was made flesh'. Hopkins used the concept of 'wording' in three senses in the poem: God making the world, his witnesses speaking his message, and the poet expressing his meaning. In stanza 29 he says that 'present and past,/Heaven and earth are word of, worded by' God; but, as in the first chapter of John, there seems to be a need for a witness to spell out and express what is there, to 'word' it, which is what the nun does in the climactic 29th stanza. Further than that, the nun's witness has to be explained, or 'worded', and this is the job of the poet and priest who, in stanza 8, which corresponds to the climax in the second part, recounts how he (among men in general) is finally brought to the point of making his statement of affirmation:

> Oh,
> We lash with the best or worst
> Word last!

The most extended parallel of the poem is that between the private

[2] Kent, Ohio, Kent State University Bulletin, 1963.

experience and the experience of the wreck, and Hopkins made this apparent when he split the poem into two parts and made them images of each other, the internal and external shipwrecks. But one must be aware of the lesser parallels of word becoming flesh, abstract becoming concrete, God becoming man, instress becoming inscape, which make the poem so full of resonances. Even the date of the death of the nuns—Hopkins includes the date in his dedication and in stanza 30 says that this was the eve of the Feast of the Immaculate Conception—adds to the sense of the miraculous which is necessary for this new wonder. The stanza form adds its associations of Incarnation since it derives some of its characteristics from Milton's stanza form in the Hymn of the Ode *On the Morning of Christ's Nativity*, a poem with which it has other interesting parallels. The first stanza concerns word being made flesh in two senses: it is on the one hand an invocation to God as Muse to inspire the poet, and on the other a realization of God's power to make and unmake generally:

> giver of breath and bread;
> World's strand, sway of the sea;
> Lord of living and dead;

and personally for Hopkins:

> Thou hast bound bones and veins in me, fastened me flesh,
> And after it almost unmade.

This twofold sense is consistent with Hopkins's theological views:

> Men of genius are said to create, a painting, a poem, a tale, a tune, a policy; not indeed the colours and the canvas, not the words or notes, but the design, the character, the air, the plan. How then?—from themselves, from their own minds. And they themselves, their minds and all, are creatures of God: if the tree created much more the flower and the fruit.   (*Sermons*, p. 238)

Stanzas 2 to 5 are an acknowledgement of his own ability to 'find' God, as he had put it in the last line of stanza 1, to recognize from experience of both terror and beauty the force behind and in the world. It is useful to use Hopkins's own terms in these stanzas, since he speaks of 'stress' in stanza 2, a 'pressure' in stanza 4, and both 'instress' and 'stress' in stanza 5. It is in these stanzas that he introduces the two sides of the effect on him of God's instress, the violent and the gentle. The abstract instress becomes the concrete inscape so that, whether it is 'lightning

and lashed rod' or the beauty of the 'dappled-with-damson west',
Hopkins can feel its effect, recognize and accept it, moving in these stanzas
from one acceptance ('I did say yes') to another ('For I greet him the
days I meet him, and bless when I understand'). The sixth and seventh
stanzas are concerned with the origin of this stress which comes, he says,
not from heaven but from the Incarnation upon which, as Scotus said,
all creation depends:

> It dates from day
> Of his going in Galilee,

which again refers to the notion of the word by recalling chapter 10 of
Acts: 'That word, I say, ye know, which was published throughout all
Judaea, and began from Galilee, after the baptism which John preached.'

The end of the seventh and the eighth stanza repeat the Incarnation
in a sexual, poetic and divine creation, each aspect wording the message
again in response to an extreme passion, either religious or secular. Even
the two stanzas addressing God and understanding his paradoxical
nature:

> Thou art lightning and love, I found it, a winter and warm;
>   Father and fondler of heart thou hast wrung:
> Hast thy dark descending and most art merciful then,

even they contain not only this movement of man towards God in
response to the movement of God towards man but also two other
examples of God's word reaching man, the sudden conversion of St
Paul and the balancing gradual conversion of St Augustine. As with
the inner group of stanzas from 2 to 5, the whole of Part the First begins
and ends on the same point, going from the almost unwilling inspiration
of 'Thou mastering me' to the eventual prayer

> Make mercy in all of us, out of us all
> Mastery, but be adored, but be adored King.

Part the Second is just as full of examples of the word being expressed
by the world, most notably in the shipwreck, which occupies the
stanzas from 12 to 17, until the poet pauses when he reaches the nun
who 'words' the meaning:

> A prophetess towered in the tumult, a virginal tongue told.

As in the first part of the poem, the poet recognizes the significance of the

terrifying experience which forces him to find expression, to 'word' it.
In stanzas 7 and 8,

> only the heart, being hard at bay,

>> Is out with it! Oh,
>> We lash with the best or worst
>> Word last!

In stanza 18 he asks,

>> make words break from me here all alone,
>> Do you!—mother of being in me, heart.

What he has to convey is that the nun has seen the instress, the force of
God, the unseeable, and he emphasizes the point by a deliberate paradox:

>> The rash smart sloggering brine
>> Blinds her; but she that weather sees one thing, one;

like Gloucester in *King Lear* she sees more clearly when she is blind,
since the revelation is not an earthly one.

Stanzas 20 to 23 are a sort of lull which separates the wreck and its
interpretation but, although they are the most easily detached and the
most easily criticized part of the poem, they elaborate on other elements
that Hopkins found in this particular shipwreck, in particular on that
information in the poem's dedication, that these were 'five Franciscan
nuns exiles by the Falck Laws'. Each piece of information here is mined
for its symbolic significance, particularly on the subject of understanding
God's message, his word. Thus in stanza 20 we see not only some
other opposites, but also the possibility, not this time of two ways of
conversion, but of two opposite responses to what Hopkins sees as God's
message. St Gertrude, a Benedictine nun, and Martin Luther stand on
opposite sides in their acceptance of the Catholic view, though they come
from the same place and have the same word available. This acceptance
or refusal of Hopkins's religion is extended in the attitude of the countries
(represented by their rivers) to the nuns in the wreck of the Deutschland,
'Rhine refused them, Thames would ruin them'. The idea surely occurs
here to prepare for the final stanza of the poem where Hopkins prays for
the return of 'Our King back, Oh, upon English souls!' The associations
of five and St Francis are elaborated in stanzas 22 and 23, again considering the relation of man to Christ and the multiple levels at which the
paradoxical aspects of grace can be realized.

After his probing of these symbols, Hopkins begins stanza 24 with a transitional comment about his own quiet thoughtfulness which could allow such lyrical expansion of the theme and, contrasting his position with the struggle out at sea, starts a lengthy exploration of this new symbol, which he finally is 'out with' in stanzas 28 and 29. The ultimate meaning is in fact where he both begins and ends, with 'the Master,/*Ipse* the only one, Christ, King, Head'. Through temporal things the nun has perceived the eternal; from the apparently 'unshapeable' scene she has with her 'single eye' gained the unified inscape, which is God. The nun is seen as repeating the role of the Virgin Mary, appropriately on the eve of the Feast of the Immaculate Conception, in that she too conceived; so that Hopkins can address the word ('the word was God and the word was with God') and say that she 'heard and kept thee and uttered thee outright'. Her action is even seen in stanza 31 as providing a way by which others in the wreck could be forgiven and come to believe. There is a frequent change of person addressed in the poem which can be confusing if it is not read carefully, but which serves to indicate movement to a new section of the poem. Stanzas 32 and 33 address God directly as the hidden 'Ground of being' whose ability to reach out is unlimited, just as the nun's message could reach even the apparently lost souls of stanza 31.

The whole wreck and the behaviour of the nun, and the poem itself, act as another Incarnation, so that stanza 34 opens by calling Christ 'new born to the world'. And the prayer at the end of the poem is addressed to the nun as well as to Christ. She, having expressed the word of God to man, is now asked to express the word of man to God. The word has not of course reached England fully in the poem, since the nun was 'at our door/Drowned', and the poem is an extension of the attempt to convey that word to 'English souls'. The message is summed up in the final line of the poem where, penetrating grammatically layer after layer, Hopkins arrives at the 'Ground of being', the meaning behind it all, 'Our hearts' charity's hearth's fire, our thoughts' chivalry's throng's Lord'. The poem ends where it began and where it reached at its climax; from 'Thou mastering me/God' to the 'King' at the end of stanza 10 by way of several acknowledgements of Christ, up to the climax in stanza 28 and on to the final 'Lord'. The whole poem seems an attempt to represent the movement between man and God, using example after example of Incarnation and man's response to it.

The central and most obvious feature of the poem's construction is its division into two parallel parts. Not that Hopkins makes a rigid parallel, as the different lengths of the parts show; he was much too subtle a man for that, and was interested not only in parallels but also in the tensions between likeness and unlikeness.

So, if one puts side by side the development of the first part and the development of the second, one has a broad similarity and important distinctions. The opening stanzas of the two parts are in strong contrast. Where stanza 1 opens the poem with life, 'giver of breath and bread', the second part opens with Death and man's ignoring of it. Yet the connections for Hopkins are obvious, in that he has pointed out in stanza 1 that God is 'Lord of living and dead', and that he too 'almost unmade' his creation. The passage that follows is in both parts of the poem the 'unmaking' stress of the wreck, stanzas 2 and 3 and stanzas 12 to 17 moving through the 'sweep and the hurl' (stanza 2), the 'horror of height' (stanza 2), or the 'hurling and horrible airs' (stanza 15) to the moment of vision when the poet boasts he is able to 'flash from the flame to the flame then, tower from the grace to the grace' (stanza 3), or the nun's actions are described as 'A prophetess towered in the tumult, a virginal tongue told' (stanza 17).

In Part the First Hopkins then spends two stanzas to widen the subject from his own moment of wreck or crisis to the more general present state, and stanzas 4 and 5 return to the present tense after the past tense of the crisis, just as stanza 18 returns to the present. In stanza 4 Hopkins uses two main images to try to convey the mysterious connection between the individual and God, another parallel on a minor scale. He is like sand or water, the one 'at the wall/Fast', the other as in a well reaching 'a poise, . . . a pane'. Both have a pattern within their seeming formlessness, the sand 'mined with a motion, a drift,/And it crowds and it combs to the fall'; while the water is connected to the streams on the hillside which are like ropes both because they look like strands down the mountain sides and because they tie him to the distant cause of his state, Christ. The two images are linked by placing them parallel but they are also mingled, rather as the events of the wreck are mingled with the poet's experience in stanzas 18 and 24; the image of the vein connects in geological terms with the 'mine' of the hourglass image, but both are connected to the veins of Christ and their redemptive blood, and the whole stanza serves to convey in physical images the strong connection with grace, 'the gospel proffer, a pressure, a principle, Christ's gift'. Another connection between the images is that Hopkins perhaps had in mind a line from a favourite poet of his, George Herbert. Herbert, in *The Collar*, speaks of being bound with a 'rope of sands'; Hopkins has the same notion of surprising coherence in apparently fragmentary material but, although he includes sand, it is his water which is 'roped'. The fifth stanza extends his sense of a fundamental principle from himself and the Welsh scenery around him to more distant things, the 'lovely-asunder Starlight' and the thunder, explaining that the presence beneath must make itself felt by being 'instressed, stressed'.

Where stanzas 4 and 5 widen the effect and speak of Hopkins's relationship with events both pleasant and awesome, stanzas 18 to 24, although they are clearly rooted in Wales, deal with Hopkins's response to the particular shipwreck, not the rather gentle recognition of the earlier stanzas, but a self-mocking awareness of his isolation from the physical danger and an exploration of the symbols of refusal of grace. These stanzas also examine the suffering caused by the refusal, both of the nuns and of Christ, and the mercy that comes from the sacrifice.

The last line of stanza 24, with its 'christens her wild-worst Best', obviously links that stanza also with stanza 8 where 'We lash with the best or worst/Word last'. And the notion of sacrifice and the Crucifixion obviously links stanzas 7 and 22. Stanzas 6 to 8, however, have a movement of argument which is matched by that of stanzas 25 to 29, namely a search for the meaning which goes through denials to assertion. Stanzas 6 to 8 insist that the gift of grace, the stress, comes not from heaven but from Christ's Incarnation and Passion, and it is this moment of extremity which releases the gift and a similar moment of extremity which acknowledges it. Similarly in stanzas 25 to 29 we learn what the nun's cry did *not* mean—it was not that she was glad to suffer as Christ had suffered, nor that she would feel the rewards more keenly because she had suffered keenly, which Hopkins says is more the sort of response of the man subject to a humdrum toil, 'The jading and jar of the cart'— before we learn what it *did* mean, namely that she in her extremity understood. Though her case and Hopkins's were vastly different, she could say with him: 'I greet him the days I meet him and bless when I understand.' Like him too in his hourglass comparison, and in many other examples of superficial movement concealing a solid ground like the shoal itself, she is 'to the blast/Tarpeïan-fast, but a blown beacon of light', combining the qualities of the rock (she has just been called 'Simon Peter of a soul') with those of a light which registers and announces the forces acting on it. She is connected to Christ again in stanza 30 by the reference to the Immaculate Conception and by the reference to both as 'light', she at the end of stanza 29, he at the beginning of stanza 30. So the last part of the poem, the nun acting as shepherd (again like Christ) for the others on the wreck, and the poem moving to an address to God and his masterful nature and a prayer that he return to England, matches the last two stanzas of the first part of the poem which mixes adoration and awe at God's mastery.

The structure of the poem, then, involves a large formal balance of two parts, but the details are no less significant and their cumulative effect is perhaps greater in knitting the fabric of the poem together. Across the large structure of repetition, there are smaller structures of repetition of words, images, syntax. There are many examples one might choose to illustrate the repetition of image, like the central idea of mastery which underlies variety. Or one could take the image of water, which as in Milton's *Lycidas* is present in both the real and a variety of symbolic senses. The majority of the stanzas have some reference to water in one form or other, from the first stanza's 'sway of the sea' to the final stanza's 'roads' and 'shoals', through a gamut of images from the 'pane' of water in stanza 4 to the very vivid and actual 'rash smart sloggering brine' of stanza 19, and including even time as a river in stanza 6. Or one could take the images of fire, flame, light, which represent both warmth and ferocity. Lightning is one aspect, the fire that allows God to forge his will (stanza 10) another; the fire may be within like the 'fire of stress' in stanza 2 or a 'lovely-asunder starlight' as in stanza 5. And often the fire is linked in a paradoxical way with its opposite: 'Though art lightning and love, I found it, a winter and warm' (stanza 9) or the 'white-fiery' snow of stanza 13. The images develop from a vast range of fires to centre on the single significance, from the acceptance in stanza 3 when he had to 'flash from the flame to the flame' or go from the 'fire of stress' to the 'all-fire glances' of stanza 23 by way of the 'Miracle-in-Mary-of-flame' of stanza 34, to that secret central comforting and finally homely fire in the last line of the poem. It is not that one image is given and then elaborated, nor that there is a mere mechanical repetition; rather Hopkins sees a variety of things in related images which grow together by the accumulation of juxta-. positions to form a unifying undercurrent to the poem. This very unity acts as an image of the single force behind all things which is an important part of his subject.

As a last example of the pervasiveness of repetitions, one can see a repetition of grammatical form used to express the difficulty in both discovering and assenting to the discovery of God in the world. In stanza 3 he uses the uncompleted, cut-off sentence when he desperately searches for a sanctuary:

> The frown of his face
> Before me, the hurtle of hell
> Behind, where, where was a, where was a place?

The puzzlement and inadequacy which this expresses is repeated in stanza 28, when he finds difficulty in grasping the proper way of making his reader realize the important thing he has to say:

> But how shall I . . . make me room there:
> Reach me a . . . Fancy, come faster—
> Strike you the sight of it? look at it loom there,
> Thing that she . . . There then!

Again the difficulties are resolved to reveal his single message, the vision of 'the Master,/*Ipse*, the only one, Christ, King, Head'. Even this discovery of the single 'ground of being' is expressed in a group of appositions. The poem, which at times, as in the ballad-like first four lines of the stanzas describing the wreck, seems to suggest it may be a narrative, is in fact a complex structure of related images and events, each of which clusters round Hopkins's central priestly theme of God's message to man and man's acceptance or denial of it.

Hopkins packed into the poem so many novelties that it still proves difficult, as it did to Coventry Patmore, the third poet among Hopkins's correspondents, who felt that 'System and learned theory are manifest in all these experiments; but they seem to me to be *too* manifest' (*Further Letters*, p. 352). Patmore's criticism still has its grain of truth:

It seems to me that the thought and feeling of these poems, if expressed without any obscuring novelty of mode, are such as often to require the whole attention to apprehend and digest them; and are therefore of a kind to appeal only to the few. But to the already sufficiently arduous character of such poetry you seem to me to have added the difficulty of following *several* entirely novel and simultaneous experiments in versification and construction, together with an altogether unprecedented system of alliteration and compound words;—any one of which novelties would be startling and productive of distraction from the poetic matter to be expressed.   (*Further Letters*, p. 352)

But when one grasps the principle of the fundamental pattern behind the surface complexity, the structure of the rhythm behind its surface variety, the interconnections of the words and images behind their surface disparity, all reflecting the single 'who and the why' behind the the apparently 'unshapeable' world, the things which Patmore complains of are in fact contributions to the effect and meaning of this extremely complex work. It is Hopkins's most complete expression of his sense of the order of the world.

3. *At Beauty Aghast*

After *The Wreck of the Deutschland* Hopkins never again wrote at such length. Although larger works were planned, most of his subsequent poetry consists of carefully-structured smaller poems. In particular the sonnet, or variations on the sonnet, gave him that measure of restriction which his ebullient invention found most congenial, providing authority and form within which he felt free to experiment. The years in Wales immediately following the writing of *The Wreck of the Deutschland* show him at his most positive in his delight in words, his meticulous wonder at Nature's variety, and his matching confidence in grasping at some unifying meaning in life. Robert Bridges accurately caught Hopkins's attitude to experience in pleasurable or painful aspect in his introductory sonnet to Hopkins's poems:

> God's terror held thee fast
> In life's wild wood at Beauty and Sorrow aghast.

It was evidently to the positive poems of the 1877 period that he was referring when he described him as 'aghast at Beauty'.

Hopkins often marks by an exclamation the very moment in the poem when he reaches this height of wonder or the point of penetrating to the significance of what he sees. So in *The Wreck of the Deutschland* three moments of this sort are clearly marked in this way: in stanza 2 'I did say yes/O at lightning and lashed rod'; in stanza 8 the heart 'Is out with it! Oh,/We lash with the best or worst/Word last!' and in stanza 29 he recognizes the nun's vision with 'Ah! there was a heart right!' So

in several of these subsequent poems we see him aghast at beauty and
marking his moment of vision by exclamation: in *God's Grandeur:*

> Oh, morning, at the brown brink eastward, springs—
> Because the Holy Ghost over the bent
> World broods with warm breast and with ah! bright wings.

Again in *The Starlight Night*:

> Look at the stars! look, look up at the skies!
> O look at all the fire-folk sitting in the air!

Again most emphatically in *The Windhover*:

> Brute beauty and valour and act, oh, air, pride, plume, here
>   Buckle!

and in the penultimate line of the same poem:

> blue-bleak embers, ah my dear,
> Fall, gall themselves, and gash gold-vermilion.

It is the power and delight with which Hopkins feels this moment of
understanding and insight, this penetration from surface to significance,
which is at the root of his poetry of this period, just as it is later the
inability to penetrate to any significance, particularly in his own life,
which is the basis of the anguish of the later poems. Throughout, Hopkins sees man's sin as obscuring the clarity of the world, thus making
perception difficult.

   Three poems from the end of this period of writing will serve to
introduce the typical interests and methods of these years. *As kingfishers
catch fire*, which dates from 1879 (or perhaps in its final form as late as
1882), is one of Hopkins's most triumphant pieces of parallelism, the
octave of the sonnet being simply eleven statements of the way in which
individual things express their own inner nature. The first four lines
are five specific examples of characteristic activity:

> As kingfishers catch fire, dragonflies draw flame;
>   As tumbled over rim in roundy wells
>   Stones ring; like each tucked string tells, each hung bell's
> Bow swung finds tongue to fling out broad its name.

Nowhere is there a better example of the idea that he had noted in his
lecture notes in 1873–4:

> there is a shape of speech possible in which there is a marked figure

and order not in the sounds but in the grammar and this might be shifted to other words with a change of specific meaning but keeping some general agreement, as of noun over against noun, verb against verb, assertion against assertion etc, e.g. Foxes (A) have (B) holes (C) and birds of the air (A′) have (B—not B′ here) nests (C′), or more widely even than this/with a change of words but keeping the grammatical and logical meaning—as/Foxes have holes and birds of the air have nests (that is/Beasts have homes to live in) but the Son of Man has not where to lay His head (that is/Man has not a home to live in): the subjects of the clauses being changed the one does no more that say yes, the other no. Hebrew poetry is said to be of this nature. This is *figure of grammar* instead of *figure of spoken sound*, which in the narrower sense is verse.   (*Journals and Papers*, p. 267)

In this poem we have examples of both the first sort of figure, King-fishers (A) catch (B) fire (C), dragonflies (A′) draw (B′) flame (C′), and the wider sort of figure where the grammatical and logical meaning is repeated. Many of Hopkins's poems can be analysed in this way. In the present poem the process continues in the second quatrain, repeating the grammatical figure, yet generalizing instead of particularizing:

> Each mortal thing does one thing and the same:
>   Deals out that being indoors each one dwells;
>   Selves—goes itself; *myself* it speaks and spells,
> Crying *What I do is me: for that I came.*

If we find a difficulty in understanding the complex line 'Deals out that being indoors each one dwells' or the novel word 'Selves', we can interpret them by comparing them with parallel statements, each meaning something like 'expresses its own essential nature'. Hopkins extends the figure even further from things to man, matching assertion against assertion, claiming that this expression of the essential nature is equivalent to becoming Christ:

> Í say more: the just man justices;
>   Keeps gráce: thát keeps all his goings graces;
>   Acts in God's eye what in God's eye he is—
>   Chríst. For Christ plays in ten thousand places,
> Lovely in limbs, and lovely in eyes not his
>   To the Father through the features of men's faces.

This is another rephrasing of what Hopkins found in Ignatius Loyola's *Spiritual Exercises*, and expressed in his comments on them:

The sun and the stars shining glorify God. They stand where he placed them, they move where he bid them. 'The heavens declare the glory of God'. They glorify God, *but they do not know it.* The birds sing to him, the thunder speaks of his terror, the lion is like his strength, the sea is like his greatness, the honey like his sweetness; they are something like him, they make him known, they tell of him, they give him glory, but they do not know they do, they do not know him, they never can, they are brute things that only think of food or think of nothing. This then is poor praise, faint reverence, slight service, dull glory. Nevertheless what they can *they always do.*

But AMIDST THEM ALL IS MAN, man and the angels: we will speak of man. Man was created. Like the rest then to praise, reverence, and serve God; to give him glory. He does so, even by his being, beyond all visible creatures . . . But man can know God, *can mean to give him glory.*   (*Sermons*, p. 239)

The ideas in that poem are also akin to those of Duns Scotus, whose writings provided for Hopkins a philosophical base and authority for his own beliefs. Somewhat against the general trend of his day, Hopkins had formulated his own theory of the individual natures of things, and it was with some delight and probably relief that he found the writings of Scotus in August of 1872:

At this time I had first begun to get hold of the copy of Scotus on the Sentences in the Baddely library and was flush with a new stroke of enthusiasm. It may come to nothing or it may be a mercy from God. But just then when I took in any inscape of the sky or sea I thought of Scotus.   (*Journals and Papers*, p. 221)

Scotus even had a word *haecceitas*, which may be translated as 'thisness', to represent the individual quality of a thing, and it is not surprising that Hopkins thought of Scotus when he took in inscapes. Nor is it surprising when one considers Scotus's ideas of creation being dependent on the Incarnation and his consequent high valuation and defence of the Virgin Mary, that Hopkins should think of the latter when he wrote *Duns Scotus's Oxford.* This poem is appropriately a reflection of the pattern of thinking which he learned from Scotus, to see a thing, realize its nature, and then perceive that nature as made distinctive by a stress behind it. The octave of the sonnet is a description of Oxford and its wedding of country and town, threatened by the souring presence of a graceless suburbia:

Towery city and branchy between towers;

Cuckoo-echoing, bell-swarmèd, lark-charmèd, rook-racked,
    river-rounded;
The dapple-eared lily below thee; that country and town did
Once encounter in, here coped and poisèd powers;

Thou hast a base and brickish skirt there, sours
That neighbour-nature thy grey beauty is grounded
Best in; graceless growth, thou hast confounded
Rural rural keeping—folk, flocks, and flowers.

Behind the intimate connection of man and nature Hopkins sees the
redeeming presence of Scotus, and marks this recognition with his
customary exclamation:

Yet ah! this air I gather and I release
He lived on; these weeds and waters, these walls are what
He haunted who of all men most sways my spirits to peace;

Of realty the rarest-veinèd unraveller; a not
Rivalled insight, be rival Italy or Greece;
Who fired France for Mary without spot.

Not only the recognition of a debt to Scotus but also the pattern of the
sonnet is important here: the description of the individual nature (perhaps
being spoiled or ignored), the recognition, and the final explanation,
dedication or prayer. In the companion poem to this, Hopkins finds his
enthusiasm for a dead composer much more vivid and real than it ever
seems for any living individual with the exception of Felix Randal.
Much more specifically in *Henry Purcell* Hopkins speaks of the individual
nature of his subject, its 'sakes', its 'forgèd feature', its 'abrupt self' which
'finds' him and brings him to his exclamation in line 9.

   The third poem which seems a useful introduction is *Binsey Poplars*,
where the reverse of the process of *As Kingfishers catch fire* saddens him.
In the kingfisher poem creation praises God unconsciously, while man
praises consciously, by choice. But the choice too often is to mar, change,
damage or frustrate the simple self-expression of nature. Where each
mortal thing of the earlier poem 'Selves—goes itself', man has marred the
scene which included the Binsey Poplars, and managed to—'unselve/The
sweet especial scene'. The effect on Hopkins, and the way in which an
event penetrated his sensibility because of its symbolic nature, can be seen
by comparing the poem with Hopkins's note in his Journal for 8 April
1873:

The ashtree growing in the corner of the garden was felled. It was lopped first: I heard the sound and looking out and seeing it maimed there came at that moment a great pang and I wished to die and not to see the inscapes of the world destroyed any more.

(Journals and Papers, p. 230)

It is not surprising that Hopkins compared the spoiling of something distinctive and 'especial' to the damage and loss of sight itself, since both involve an inability to see the self of the thing looked at.

In these poems one can find the core of Hopkins's poetry of this period, the search for the nature of the object, the pattern of the poem, and the recognition of man's tendency to refuse to see and to mar that nature. Of course not all of these are strongly evident in every poem. Take Hopkins's favourite sonnet, which tends to have much fanciful commentary from critics. Its direct subject is the grasping of the nature of a falcon, Hopkins using the word 'caught' not only because it is more active on the part of the beholder than 'saw' but also because it represents his activity reflecting and fired by that of the falcon. The kingfisher had 'caught fire'; in his Journal for 24 May 1871 Hopkins had written a note which suggests the way in which catching fire unites disparate objects:

It was a glowing yellow sunset. Pendle and all the hills rinsed clear, their heights drawn with a brimming light, in which windows or anything that could catch fluttered and laughed with the blaze.

(Journals and Papers, p. 210)

and one remembers the fire images in The Wreck of the Deutschland. Thus the first two words of the poem include an undercurrent which, links to the last two lines, where the embers, breaking open to reveal their fiery heart, suggest the sacrifice of Christ. This connection is fully in keeping with Hopkins's efforts to make his poems themselves have a shape, a carefully-integrated construction of rhythm, grammar and image, in other words their own inscape. This is quite as important as his justly-admired success in the octave of this sonnet in representing the movement of the flight in the movement of the verse. The pattern of the poem recalls that of Duns Scotus's Oxford. The octave describes the bird, and the sestet begins by recognizing what it signifies. The falcon 'goes itself' by a combination or 'buckling' of 'Brute beauty and valour and act, oh, air, pride, plume'. But these things buckle in another sense too, in that they give under the pressure and, as happened under pressure in The Wreck of the Deutschland, they utter Christ. His response to the bird, from

his place 'in hiding' as he had been away from the wreck in the earlier
poem, is significantly to its 'mastery'. To see its inscape means to see the
amazing extra element of Christ in it or his fire; no wonder that Hopkins
should stress the importance of this additional blessing by putting his
'AND' in capital letters. The further explanations of the last three lines
repeat the point that any duty done will be acting 'in God's eye what in
God's eye he is—/Christ'. The dedication 'To Christ our Lord' is not only
because the poem addresses Christ in line 11, but also because it is
concerned with the Christlike activity of all things.

Pied Beauty is much less complex, but still deals with nature praising
God and the poet choosing to praise. It retains the proportions but
shortens the length of a normal sonnet to make what Hopkins called a
'Curtal sonnet'. Beginning with praise, it builds up through a description
of a variety of beautiful things which either are 'pied' or contain opposites
of various kinds—colour, taste, speed, brightness—to an assertion of the
Creator of them, whose ability to comprehend the paradoxes within
his unity aptly demands praise, which ends the poem with a formal
perfection by returning to its beginning. The poem differs from The
Wreck of the Deutschland, which also dealt with paradoxical appearances
behind which God was the 'ground of being', in that all the opposites
here are pleasant, and the effect happily positive.

The same effect comes from the most gladly ecstatic of his poems,
Hurrahing in Harvest, The one harvest around him inspires him to glean
another, and his eyes and heart receive direct replies of Christ's being in
the universe. In fact the things he sees are Christ:

> And the azurous hung hills are his world-wielding shoulder
> Majestic—as a stallion stalwart, very-violet-sweet!

The message is the same as before, that man merely has to learn to look
with his heart and eyes to see these causes for such joy that he can half
partake in their unearthliness:

> these things were here and but the beholder
> Wanting; which two when they once meet,
> The heart rears wings bold and bolder
> And hurls for him, O half hurls earth for him off under his feet.

The Caged Skylark is almost an explanation of why he wrote 'half hurls';
not because he is cynically aware of his inability to forget he is human,
but because his humanity can be transformed partly as it will be fully.

Like the caged skylark, he reacts against his confines, aspires above them and is frustrated by them, but he argues that

> Man's spirit will be flesh-bound when found at best,
> But uncumberèd.

The process of beholding and gaining to the state of joy is of course for Hopkins one of prayer and service, as he frequently states in his sermons and notes; but it is equally part of his poetry. Both *The Starlight Night* and *Spring* concern this priestly theme, though they both open with descriptions, made up as usual of a series of parallels including the familiar fire image between images found elsewhere of gold and doves:

> The grey lawns cold where gold, where quickgold lies!
> Wind-beat whitebeam! airy abeles set on a flare!
> Flake-doves sent floating forth at a farmyard scare!

The parallels which illustrate the assertion that 'Nothing is so beautiful as Spring' are expressive of Hopkins's love of individuality, of exuberant nonconformity, but equally have that unifying undertone linking them on a philosophic and a semantic level. It is nature's lavishness uninterfered with by man which comes out most strongly in his first picture of the 'weeds, in wheels, shoot long and lovely and lush'. But the senses are so sharpened that small and great things have equal and enormous impact: eggs become heavens, the thrush's song 'strikes like lightnings', the pear-tree comes into contact with the sky, and the sky itself becomes full of life like the egg 'all in a rush/With richness'. The repetition is not only of structure here, but of idea, everything involved in activity, not only of growing but even the mundane household chores of cleaning in 'rinse and wring' and 'brush' as if involved in a cosmic and spiritual spring cleaning. The lamb, as a familiar image of the innocent member of the flock and of Christ, makes a clear link with the second part of the poem where Hopkins relates 'all this juice and all this joy' to 'A strain of the earth's sweet being in the beginning/In Eden garden' and to the innocence of the Virgin Mary and Christ. In a rather difficult sentence, he asks Christ to get this innocence before it is lost, presumably while the children are still innocent or, as with nature, after a spiritual cleaning to acquire innocence. May, associated with Mary ('May is Mary's month', wrote Hopkins in *The May Magnificat*), is also referred to in *The Starlight Night*, where the description in the octave is followed by encouragement to buy and bid for the revealed joys and incidentally for innocence with 'Prayer, patience, alms, vows'.

'Souring with sinning' and man's destruction of his once pure world come more clearly into other poems, which nonetheless relate clearly to the poems of glad recognition. *God's Grandeur* again links the fire image—'It will flame out'—with the confession of God under pressure—'like the ooze of oil/Crushed'. But it also considers how man has refused to recognize the element of God in everything. Indeed, the words that Hopkins chooses indicate the sense of sameness and the lack of distinctiveness which man has imposed upon his world:

> Generations have trod, have trod, have trod;
>> And all is seared with trade; bleared, smeared with toil;
>> And wears man's smudge and shares man's smell: the soil
> Is bare now, nor can foot feel, being shod.

Despite this obvious displeasure at man's unwillingness to recognize what he has obscured, the poem reverts to the pattern of the happier poems, seeing a renewal almost like that of spring after winter, or a new day, or a new egg-like promise of life under the brooding Holy Ghost:

> And for all this, nature is never spent;
>> There lives the dearest freshness deep down things;
>> And though the last lights off the black West went
>> Oh, morning, at the brown brink eastward, springs—
> Because the Holy Ghost over the bent
>> World broods with warm breast and with ah! bright wings.

This last line, uniting the 'bright wings' of exultation and discovery with the brooding and protecting wings of care, connects the poem with many others which bear witness to his keen and sympathetic observation of birds. *The Wreck of the Deutschland* had its 'dovewinged' heart, the protective 'feathers' of the Father, and the 'feathery delicacy' of Providence; *The Windhover* is based on the mastery of the bird's flight, and there are many others where bird song, bird flight, the colour of birds' wings or birds' eggs, or the nesting of birds provide his imagery.

The homely comforts he received and recorded in *In the Valley of the Elwy* suggest to him that the 'cordial air' made a hood for 'those kind people'

> All over, as a bevy of eggs the mothering wing
> Will, or mild nights the new morsels of Spring.

As in *God's Grandeur* it is 'Only the inmate does not correspond', and the only remedy to pray that God should 'Complete thy creature dear O where it fails'. *The Sea and the Skylark* uses the two aspect of its title to show how both pure natural things express their character, in contrast to man who is losing his identity and destroying his pattern:

> . . . We, life's pride and cared-for crown,
>   Have lost that cheer and charm of earth's past prime:
> Our make and making break, are breaking, down
>   To man's last dust, drain fast towards man's first slime.

The Sea and the Skylark is distinctive among this early group in ending on the note of loss much more emphatically than *Binsey Poplars*. Hopkins is more likely at this time to see even the apparent desertion of man as functional, as when, continuing the bird imagery in *Peace*, he reconciles himself to thinking that the occasional peace he feels is amply supplied by patience which, like the mothering bird, is necessary to the growth of the young into its full plumage. It is a functional patience, not a comfortable peace, and has obvious connections with the experience in *Patience, hard thing!*

> O surely, reaving Peace, my Lord should leave in lieu
> Some good! And so he does leave Patience exquisite,
> That plumes to Peace thereafter. And when Peace here does house
> He comes with work to do, he does not come to coo,
>   He comes to brood and sit.

There is a similar sense of patiently accepting apparent abandonment in the slightly less successful *Andromeda*, where the abandonment is of the Church in general rather than the poet in particular. The Church, as Hopkins pictures it, is Andromeda bound to the rock and threatened by an unprecedented menace. The threat obviously includes Protestantism (Luther was called 'beast of the waste wood' in *The Wreck of the Deutschland*) and—even more unpleasant for Hopkins—the rationalism and atheism of his day, combined with all those other gestures of denial in 'our sordid, turbid time'. As in *Peace*, Hopkins sees this as only the apparent situation; Andromeda seems forsaken, but this is merely a trial of patience which 'comes with work to do', and she will be released from her enemies unexpectedly, her Perseus disarming both with beauty and power, both paradoxical qualities expressed in one word and thus expressing their co-presence in Christ.

There is no complete rejection of man, despite the sometimes gloomy awareness of his refusal to follow what Hopkins saw as the right way. *The Lantern out of Doors* praises just those who do have some physical or intellectual beauty:

> Men go by me whom either beauty bright
> In mould or mind or what not else makes rare:

and they do have, despite his inability to follow them, some effect:

> They rain against our much-thick and marsh air
> Rich beams, till death or distance buys them quite.

Hopkins's own inability to follow them is made up for by Christ's care and company, which goes with them through distance and death. The poem is a companion piece to *The Candle Indoors*, which again deals with his own response to light putting back darkness. Here, however, seeing a candle putting back the dark, he wishes the occupant of the house to be engaged in some task in a way which will glorify God, equally putting back the dark. But in this poem the poet turns upon his own inadequacy much more fiercely than he had done in stanza 18 of *The Wreck of the Deutschland*. Taking his imagery from two parts of the Sermon on the Mount, he mocks his own imperfections in Christ's words to his disciples in Matthew, chapter 5: 'Ye are the salt of the earth: but if the salt have lost his savour, wherewith shall it be salted? it is thenceforth good for nothing, but to be cast out, and to be trodden under foot of men.' The passage about the candle and the advice to shine before men follow this passage, and Hopkins was obviously familiar with these lines from the seventh chapter of Matthew: 'Thou hypocrite, first cast out the beam out of thine own eye; and then shalt thou see clearly to cast out the mote out of thy brother's eye.' In wondering whether he was not in fact salt that had spent its savour, Hopkins had begun that movement towards the agonizing self-exploration which we find in his later poems.

His poetry following *The Wreck of the Deutschland* had extended the argument from that poem to a discovery of God working in natural things, his message available to innocent, pure, patient and praising men, but ignored by humanity in general. It was when Hopkins began to consider his own inefficiency in doing anything about it that his poetry began to change significantly.

4. *At Sorrow Aghast*

It is mainly for convenience that I make a division between the positive poems of discovering God in the world and the negative poems of the difficulty of finding him. There is always the undercurrent of the opposite feeling in Hopkins's work, often even within the same word, and his experience was by no means compartmentalized so rigidly. For example, a nightmare is recorded in the Journals in 1873, a time before any of the major poems was written, while the poem which relates to it dates from 1885, only four years before his death. And as Professor Mackenzie points out in the Foreword to the Fourth Edition of Hopkins's poems (p. xlviii), the same sheet of paper which bears *To seem the stranger lies my lot*, *I wake and feel the fell of dark*, *Patience, hard thing!*, and *My own heart let me more have pity on*, also contains the lines which Robert Bridges called *Ashboughs*. In these lines Hopkins is again interested in the relationship between the earthly and the heavenly, and uses the ash as the link between them as earlier he had used the falcon, harvest, or the peartree in *Spring*, which relates closely to this poem:

> Not of all my eyes see, wandering on the world,
> Is anything a milk to the mind so, so sighs deep
> Poetry tó it, as a tree whose boughs break in the sky.
> Say it is áshboughs: whether on a December day and furled
> Fast ór they in clammyish lashtender combs creep
> Apart wide and new-nestle at heaven most high.

> They touch heaven, tabour on it; how their talons sweep
> The smouldering enormous winter welkin! May
> Mells blue and snowwhite through them, a fringe and fray
> Of greenery: it is old earth's groping towards the steep
>   Heaven whom she childs us by.

The sense of delight is still here, just as in the earlier poems there are bleak passages qualifying the shouts of joy.

There is a noticeable changing in the poetry from the earlier happier years in Wales to the sadder years when he felt weighed down by his experiences in Liverpool and his work in Ireland. Although it had been implicit in his early work, sadness becomes explicit in *Peace*, *The Candle Indoors*, and in such a tender poem as *Spring and Fall*. According to the title it is addressed 'to a young child', but the movement is not only towards her mourning for herself, but also towards Hopkins's mourning for himself. He becomes the 'fall' to her 'spring' and the contrast of youth and age, innocence and experience, is at the basis of this finely-modulated poem, in some ways a miniature *Tintern Abbey*. The first two lines question and wonder that the child can be sad about a wood's loss of leaves, however beautiful and valuable the wood that 'Golden-grove' summons up. Picking up the word 'leaves' in the third line,

Hopkins extends the question to suggest the ability of the innocent girl to care for things both of nature and of man. The form of the question is suddenly created by the last two words of the fourth line, which helps to represent the observer's sense of wonder:

> Márgarét, áre you gríeving
> Over Goldengrove unleaving?
> Leáves, líke the things of man, you
> With your fresh thoughts care for, can you?

The freshness of the girl's thoughts is important, for it is in direct opposition to the poet's older and colder heart, which is, like the leaves and the season and man, fallen. The next four lines balance the first four, the inability to feel for natural things being the inevitable consequence of age for Hopkins as it was for Wordsworth:

> Áh! ás the heart grows older
> It will come to such sights colder
> By and by, nor spare a sigh
> Though worlds of wanwood leafmeal lie.

Hopkins's lively inventiveness with words, putting together 'wan' and 'wood' to make a pale autumnal equivalent of 'Goldengrove' and making 'leafmeal' on analogy with 'piecemeal', does not obscure his meaning but rather intensifies the impression of the great change that comes about between spring and fall. Line 9 marks the turning point in the poem: in terms of rhyme it seems to belong with the couplet before it, yet its meaning contradicts it; in its weeping it belongs to the first four lines, but in its cause of weeping to the second four; in its weeping it seems to relate to spring, but it is knowledge as in Adam's case which causes the weeping: 'And yet you *will* weep and know why.' He then, as someone who knows why he weeps, explains, contrasting the future of 'you *will* weep' with the present 'Now'. To the child the name is unimportant, since there are no distinctions between the things of nature and the things of man, but the name in fact reinforces the point by insisting in a pun that for innocent and knowing alike falls are the springs of sorrow. Spring and fall are thus the same, and the child's heart and spirit had recognized the common cause of sorrow without being able to express it verbally or even to realize it. In this she reminds us of a passage in I Corinthians ii:

Eye hath not seen, nor ear heard, neither have entered into the heart of man, the things which God hath prepared for them that love him. . . . For what man knoweth the things of a man, save the spirit of man which is in him?

And one might also be reminded of Wordsworth's *Immortality Ode* where the child is an

> Eye among the blind,
> That, deaf and silent, read'st the eternal deep,
> Haunted for ever by the eternal mind.

The poet with all his fallen knowledge can find the words and for Hopkins the cause is simple:

> It ís the blight man was born for,
> It is Margaret you mourn for.

The series of balances and comparisons in this poem give it a calm but persuasive articulation, and the consciousness of all that is involved in 'knowledge' and 'fall' give this apparently slight poem a great deal of weight.

Before the later poems which show fully his agonized consciousness of his place as fallen man, Hopkins was occupied with his drama of St Winefred, and his poems for a while show his concern for working out what man could do to escape the dismal consequence of the fall, and how his own activity in particular could be significant. This explains a group of poems in which he is concerned with man's search for permanence, for Hopkins a possibility only in God. *The Leaden Echo and the Golden Echo*, which is the Maidens' song from *St. Winefred's Well*, gives the basic question and answer: 'Is there any key to keep beauty from vanishing away? Yes. Give beauty back to God.' It is on this basic formula that the whole poem is orchestrated in an elaborate series of parallels, a tumbling tune of synonyms and appositions. One could set out the first passage like this to represent its equations, the sentence running normally from left to right but the equivalents arranged in columns:

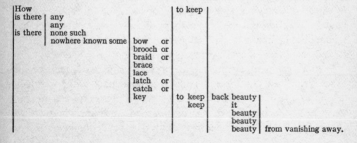

The following sentence repeats the same question, suggesting ways to keep beauty from vanishing away; and the whole poem is an extreme example of the way Hopkins builds through balances of syntax and idea, linking all the time with echoes of sound in consonants and vowels, as in that series of words implying both decoration and restraint, 'bow or brooch or braid or brace, lace, latch or catch or key' which finally modulates to the verb 'keep'. Hopkins felt that he 'never did anything more musical' (*Correspondence*, p. 149), and Christopher Devlin rightly remarks that there is a 'perfect fusion of his spiritual sensuousness and his religious ideals; they [the choruses in the poem] were in the high tradition of the seventeenth-century refusal to let beauty and morality go different ways' (*Sermons*, p. 215). One might well say the same of Hopkins's answer to his own question, *To what serves Mortal Beauty*, which is to accept it and thus God in it:

> Merely meet it; own,
> Home at heart, heaven's sweet gift; ' then leave, let that alone.
> Yea, wish that though, wish all, ' God's better beauty, grace.

Hopkins's own satisfaction in those he saw acting beautifully or dedicating beauty to God, even his satisfaction in those he helped by ministering to them, does not always make for powerful poetry. *The Handsome Heart* has elements which work strongly in *The Wreck of the Deutschland*—the homing-pigeon instinct of the heart and the loving subservience to the will of the Father—but the prayer that the boy keep on this virtuous path does not disguise the rather Victorian sentimentality of the picture. Similarly with *The Bugler's First Communion*; despite its pleasant tone of banter in its forwardness with heaven and despite its intriguing technical experiments, the poem does not rise above its particular occasion to justify its complexity. Nor does *Brothers*, with its limiting story, manage 'Wordsworth's manner' as he had hoped. *Morning, Midday, and Evening Sacrifice*, however, with its eager advice to render to God the qualities of youth, prime, and age, each in a separate stanza, manages to catch something of the spirit of Hopkins's belief, earnest, complete, solicitous and vigorous.

Felix Randal stands out among the poems of Hopkins's ministry with some force. Not only does it register his delight at being spiritually helpful to one of his parishioners, but it also contrives to recognize the individuality of the man while presenting him as an almost heroic type. His attitude too seems to be something of that wondering love and awe

with which he regarded nature earlier and which he recommends in
To what serves Mortal Beauty, rather than the indulgent condescension
with which he looks at the *Brothers* or the boy of *The Handsome Heart*.
If Felix Randal had something of the childlike innocence which Hopkins
found so attractive, this is won by the man with the help of the priest. It
is the joy at the part he played in this process from fallen man to redeemed
innocence which Hopkins conveys most strongly. Again the poem
progresses through contrasts, the two quatrains of the octave depicting
the movement from strength to weakness in his huge physical presence,
and from weakness to strength in his spiritual condition. This is emphasized by the use of 'mended' in line 5:

> Sickness broke him. Impatient, he cursed at first, but mended.

The word is used in Lancashire of someone getting better from illness,
and Hopkins, writing in Lancashire of an ordinary man, used the local
'and all' and 'all road ever' and 'fettle' as appropriate to his subject. The
implications of 'mended' are that his spiritual condition did indeed
improve in contrast to his physical, so that the movement of the lines is
aptly from news of his death in line 1, through sickness of body, improve-
ment of spiritual health to prayer for rest whatever his sins. The 'seeing
the sick' of line 9 thus suggests the twofold meaning of sickness in this
case, and for Hopkins the spiritual cure had been something which
made him too richer and more worthy:

> This seeing the sick endears them to us, us too it endears.
> My tongue had taught thee comfort, touch had quenched thy tears,
> Thy tears that touched my heart, child, Felix, poor Felix Randal.

He had been the agent of Felix Randal's recovery of childlike innocence,
yet the poem is saved from merely seeming a portrait of touching
usefulness because it turns in its last three lines back to the prime of his
life when the farrier is at work, without conscious thought performing
his activity. As Hopkins wrote in his notes:

> It is not only prayer that gives God glory but work. Smiting on an
> anvil, sawing a beam, whitewashing a wall, driving horses, sweeping,
> scouring, everything gives God some glory if being in his grace you
> do it as your duty.   (*Sermons*, p. 240)

Thus the apparent turn from the spiritual to the physical again is rather
a method of seeing Felix Randal as in both aspects of his life fulfilling

his duty—it is significantly his own duty to which Hopkins refers in the first line, rather than to his love. The duty of shoeing that the farrier performs is resonant with echoes of other of Hopkins's poems: God in *The Wreck of the Deutschland* 'With an anvil-ding/And with fire' forged his will in man (stanza 10); the grey of ordinary life appeared in stanza 26 of the same poem; Christ's shoulder is seen as 'as a stallion stalwart' in *Hurrahing in Harvest*; and the spark-making blows of the horse's shod hooves suggest the idea that, as in *St. Alphonsus Rodriguez*, 'Honour is flashed off exploit'. Felix Randal's mortal beauty had a function as much as his subsequent spiritual beauty, and it is this completeness of the man, his antithetical but not mutually exclusive qualities, which Hopkins manages to capture, leaving the reader with the strength and beauty of the last image.

No other poem records such success in his priestly function or such delight in a fellow man. Otherwise most of his heroes are saints, his men mostly sinners, his children dear innocents who will all too soon fall, and he himself most consciously a failure. His self-lacerating question and demand to put his own house in order in *The Candle Indoors*, and the awareness of 'the blight man was born for', lead to a group of poems perhaps best thought of as the *negative* poems, to match the positive affirmations of the earlier group. Here the poet sees himself as failure, and fails to see God's purpose in him; it is as if he loses an understanding of his own design, his own inscape. Two extracts from his Journals show how he looked at his difficulties. One concerns the outer world, the state of the College at Stonyhurst:

> candles in bottles, things not ready, darkness and despair. In fact being unwell I was quite downcast: nature in all her parcels and faculties gaped and fell apart, *fatiscebat*, like a clod cleaving and holding only by strings of root. But this must often be.
>
> (*Journals and Papers*, p. 236)

The feeling of loss of unity is even more terrible when it is of the self, as as it seemed to be a month later:

> I had a nightmare that night. I thought something or someone leapt onto me and held me quite fast: this I think woke me, so that after this I shall have had the use of reason. This first start is, I think, a nervous collapse of the same sort as when one is very tired and holding oneself at stress not to sleep yet/suddenly goes slack and seems to fall and wakes, only on a greater scale and with a loss of muscular control

reaching more or less deep; this one to the chest and not further, so that I could speak, whispering at first, then louder—for the chest is the first and greatest centre of motion and action, the seat of θυμός. I had lost all muscular stress elsewhere but not sensitive, feeling where each limb lay and thinking that I could recover myself if I could move my finger, I said, and then the arm and so the whole body. The feeling is terrible: the body no longer swayed as a piece by the nervous and muscular instress seems to fall in and hang like a dead weight on the chest. I cried on the holy name and by degrees recovered myself as I thought to do. It made me think that this was how the souls in hell would be imprisoned in their bodies as in prisons and of what St. Theresa says of her 'little press in the wall' where she felt herself to be in her vision.   (*Journals and Papers*, p. 238)

There are several points to bring out from this note. First, that it dates from before the period of the positive poems. Second, that it represents a period of crisis, but not one which abandons hope in God. Third, that he acknowledges that 'this must often be'. Fourth, that he expresses the terrible feeling as a loss of 'nervous and muscular instress'. Last, that although the note is early, the poem which most clearly draws on this experience is *I wake and feel the fell of dark*.

This poem is almost the reverse of the positive poems. It begins with eight lines attempting to realize and depict the nature of his loss of unity, his loss of meaning and light. In a sense the poem must have been consoling in forcing at least an artistic unity on the fragmenting experience, yet the experience is all of frustration and negation. The opening line expects day and finds 'not day', he wakes with an expectation of seeing but only feels, and what he feels is all those associations of wild animal, suddeness, falling, which cluster round the notion of the 'fell of dark'. The sights witnessed in these 'black hours', as in the 'darkness visible' which lit up the doleful sights of hell for the damned in *Paradise Lost*, are not at an end. Day does not come, although in *St. Winefred's Well* Hopkins had used 'sure as to-morrow morning' as an example of 'what is most sure'. The climactic frustration is the unavailability to him of God, who not only lives far away, but never receives any of the letters sent:

> And my lament
> Is cries countless, cries like dead letters sent
> To dearest him that lives alas! away.

Nonetheless, this pattern is to Hopkins some sort of consolation in that it at least gives him an identity which corresponds to 'God's most deep decree', and he has the example of St Theresa. The consolation, that he is better than the damned, is desperate but behind it all is his determined faith, his willed belief.

The hell of the last lines recalls an equivalent hell in *Spelt from Sibyl's Leaves*, where he becomes aware

<blockquote>
of a rack
Where, selfwrung, selfstrung, sheathe- and shelterless, '
thóughts agaínst thoughts ín groans grínd.
</blockquote>

It is significant that the delight in variety of the positive poems has dwindled to a recognition of only two 'spools', 'flocks' or 'folds' into which the 'once skéined stained véined varíety' must be divided; the artistic variety struggles much more desperately with the moral singleness of choice. The source of the gloomy message to consider right and wrong only is expressed in the octave of the sonnet, for indeed this is a sonnet, despite the fact that each line has eight stresses, making it according to Hopkins 'the longest sonnet ever made' (*Letters*, p. 245). Hopkins had always read 'tales' or 'oracles' in nature, but the messages were growing darker. Here evening becomes night, the variety of the world becomes mixed and indistinguishable and the stars become not lights but observing fires. Again, the waning of life, the fall, is seen as a loss of unifying and distinguishing elements: the lights of the third line become 'Waste', the 'being' of earth is 'unbound' as when he was ill at Stonyhurst, 'her dapple is at an end', everything mixed up together 'all throughther', and the self lost in other selves. This loss of self can still bring out his delight in word to challenge it by defining the very self of the loss, so that the process of 'disremembering' or forgetting is seen alongside the process of cutting to pieces, dismembering; so that though oblivion is loss of self and unity, the two are paradoxically connected together by their sound. As usual, Hopkins has picked up the local word to help him, this time an Irish one, though he had picked up other words from Lancashire and Wales.

The darkness and the sense of threat in this poem are characteristic of this period where he seems to be turning to those ultimate distinctions of black and white. Frightening as it might be, Hopkins was in some ways familiar with ultimate distinctions, more familiar perhaps than with ordinary men and women. One of his central qualities, an ability to see clearly into fundamental issues, has as its obverse an occasional inability to see clearly into human failing, above all his own failing, with compassion. Some retreat notes of 1888, from which I extract only parts, show his fierce rigour with himself:

I am now 44. I do not waver in my allegiance, I never have since my conversion to the Church. The question is how I advance the side I serve on. This may be inwardly or outwardly. Outwardly I often think I am employed to do what is of little or no use. . . . I do not feel then that outwardly I do much good, much that I care to do or can much wish to prosper; and this is a mournful life to lead. In thought I can of course divide the good from the evil and live for the one, not the other: this justifies me, but it does not alter the facts. Yet it seems to me that I could lead this life well enough if I had bodily energy and cheerful spirits. However these God will not give me. The other part, the more important, remains, my inward service.

I was continuing this train of thought this evening when I began to enter on that course of loathing and hopelessness which I have so often felt before, which made me fear madness and led me to give up the practice of meditation except, as now, in retreat, and here it is again. I could therefore do no more than repeat *justus es, Domine, et rectum judicium tuum* and the like, and then being tired I nodded and woke with a start. What is my wretched life? Five wasted years almost have passed in Ireland. I am ashamed of the little I have done, of my waste of time, although my helplessness and weakness is such that I could scarcely do otherwise. And yet the wise man warns us against excusing ourselves in that fashion. I cannot then be excused; but what is life without aim, without spur, without help? All my undertakings miscarry: I am like a straining eunuch. I wish then for death: yet if I died now I shd. die imperfect, no master of myself, and that is the worst picture of all. O my God, look down on me.

(*Further Letters*, pp. 447–8)

The Sonnets of Desolation, the negative poems, show his struggle with these problems, and though they indeed represent a recogniton of failures and negative qualities in himself, they are on the other hand dramatically positive efforts to struggle with his difficulties.

Only two of the sonnets end without a direct countering of despair. *No worst, there is none* seems to find no comfort but the periodic 'lull' in his cries, and the desperate comfort of the end of day and the end of life. Nothing seems more vivid than the limitlessness of grief, pangs, cries, fall; and nothing more limited that 'our small durance' and comfort. Perhaps he gains some comfort in the last line from the acknowledgement of the finiteness of the world as opposed to the infinity of eternity, as if this poem begins where *I wake and feel the fell of dark* ends. Certainly *To seem the stranger lies my lot* could be said to have two comforts, first the recognition of some function, his 'lot' even though an unpleasant one, and second the admission that he 'can/Kind love both give and get'. But it ends thwarted. In both these poems, however, the poem itself is a counter to despair. Where in the earlier poems the complex pattern of the form and sound reflects the pattern of the thing observed, in these later poems the form is itself a struggle to impose an order on a disintegrating life. Instead of being an echo of the sense, the poems are the very process of asserting a structure on unwilling material, a struggle which gives the poems much of their strength.

Carrion Comfort, for example, counters the approach of despair with willed effort. Amongst the flood of negatives in the first four lines stands out the simple assertion 'I can', which finds support from the double negative 'not choose not to be', which stubbornly turns the temptation to negation back on despair and refuses what the first three lines have expressed, the temptation 'not to be'. The fight in this poem is not solely with despair, because the fifth line is addressed to God who, as in stanza 2 of *The Wreck of the Deutschland*, is controlling the 'tempest' which Hopkins is 'frantic to avoid'. The movement of the rest of the poem has its parallels in those early stanzas of *The Wreck of the Deutschland*, and is another 'saying yes to God'. The tempest is no longer in the sestet to be avoided, but a purgation, a sifting, a flailing 'That my chaff might fly; my grain lie, sheer and clear', and it is also a source of strength in that the 'wrestling' was an act for which he can now cheer both God and himself, just as he could delight that the storm brought praise to God and the nun in the poem on the wreck. The exclamation 'my God!' in the last line is characteristic of Hopkins's ability to make a commonplace work for him: it marks his amazement in its ordinary usage; it marks his deeper wonder that he has in truth been struggling with his God; and it registers that God is in fact his in a very personal way.

Patience, hard thing! counters the approach of despair with faith and argument, with knowledge of religious example, and with an image. As he had said in *The Starlight Night*, what one must bid in order to buy delights is 'Prayer, patience, alms, vows'. Patience here involves not simple inactivity, but war, wounds, weariness and defeats; no wonder he finds it hard to pray for, which he sees as the best obedience. The first comfort he allows himself is the image of the ivy. This roots in those earlier aspects of patience and, in covering the ruins of other hopes, finds a necessary place to support its berries and feel the sun. There is a good deal going on in lines 5 to 8. Patience needs the place to root and can root in nothing else; it masks the wreckage of past purpose, but it also depends on it to feel the sun and warmth that give it life. The paradoxical nature of this relationship is brought out by the shipwreck reference, since it is the 'seas of liquid leaves' which depend on the 'wrecked past purpose' for support; the wrecked purpose upholds its wrecking element. The 'purple eyes' of the ivy are both beautiful berries full of life and the results of taking tosses in the fight, a reference which leads naturally on to the 'bruise them dearer' of line 10. Lines 9 to 11 return to the determined obedience and the images of war and stress of the first four lines, 'grate', 'kills,' 'bruise', 'bend', images which are reminiscent of Donne's struggles with God:

> That I may rise and stand, o'erthrow me and bend
> Your force to break, blow, burn and make me new.

In contrast to this prayer for violence, however, the last three lines of Hopkins's poem reach for the gentle imagery of the second quatrain, the association of honey gathered from the flowers opened to the sun; patience, rooted in struggles with despair, supported in the sunshine upon the resulting wreckage, becomes the honey which God distils and which he returns to the man who awaits grace in patience. While the balance which the rhyme emphasizes is between quatrain and quatrain and between tercet and tercet, there are other cross-linkings, and a thread of argument continuing through the poem to balance the hardness of patience with the sweetness of patience at the end.

Almost as an example of patience, a calm acceptance making for sanctity, Hopkins wrote a sonnet on *St. Alphonsus Rodriguez*. Although it was in fact 'written to order', Hopkins used the opportunity to depict a man in the Society of Jesus who carried out that 'inward service' which he himself found so difficult yet did so fully. The sonnet, he wrote in a letter to Bridges, '(I say it snorting) aims at being intelligible' (*Letters*, p. 293). The argument is indeed quite simple, contrasting the 'war without', where heroic martyrdoms and fighting for the cause provide obvious honour, with the 'war within' which seems to go unheard. The turn in the sestet at 'Yet' has been implied by the 'so we say' of the first line, which Hopkins explained in a letter as 'This is what we commonly say, but we are wrong' (*Letters*, p. 297). In keeping with his thought about the opposing aspects of God, as hewer of vast shapes and gentle instigator of growth in both the tiny and huge aspects of nature, Hopkins sees God as able to make the 'war within' significant even when the life seems 'without event':

> Yet God . . .
> Could crowd career with conquest while there went
> Those years and years by of world without event
> That in Majorca Alfonso watched the door.

The application to Hopkins's own situation and longing for significance is evident.

Two other poems of this period deal with individuals, though neither deals particularly with the character of the man, *Harry Ploughman* concerned largely with his appearance, and *Tom's Garland* with his place in society. Hopkins sent them to Dixon with the comments that they were

> works of infinite, of over great contrivance, I am afraid, to the an-
> nulling in the end of the right effect. They have also too much resem-
> blance to each other; but they were conceived at the same time. They
> are of a 'robustious' sort.   (*Correspondence*, p. 153)

Their similarity is in their view of the whole being made up of parts in their appropriate places, Tom being part of the Commonwealth whose health lies in having a place for all and whose sickness in having those who do not share its prosperity, and Harry himself being composed of parts each of which is a member of 'one crew' and has a proper 'rank' and function. Intriguing as these poems are, with Harry Ploughman having almost a combination of 'Brute beauty and valour and act', they do not reach the delight in individuality as roundly as earlier poems, and they lack the simplicity of argument which allows others of Hopkins's poems to support a complexity of detail. One eventually comes to the same sort of conclusion as those that Hopkins himself came to: of *Tom's Garland* in particular, though the point may well apply also to *Harry Ploughman*, that 'I think that it is a very pregnant sonnet and in point of execution very highly wrought. Too much so, I am afraid'; and that 'It is plain I must go no farther on this road' (*Letters*, pp. 274 and 272).

The poems, no less than the letters and Journals and meditations, show him as his own most stringent critic, and the image of the self grinding on the self is repeated, from the hell in the last line of *Spelt from Sibyl's Leaves* to *St. Alphonsus Rodriguez* and the 'war within'. A welcome respite comes in *My own heart let me more have pity on*, where he counters the approach of despair with faith and imagery as he had done in *Patience, hard thing!*, though reflecting the tormenting involutions of the mind in a churning effect of syntax and repetitions. The balance between quatrain and quatrain and tercet and tercet are similar to those of *Patience, hard thing!*, but this time the first four lines are the charitable straightforward statements, the second four using the imagery to picture his comfortless state. Even there, however, the logic of the images demonstrates his faith, since the day is there even if the blind man cannot see it and water can be available as it was to the Ancient Mariner when he allowed himself to bless. Comfort must be allowed 'root-room' like patience, and he advises himself in his ordinary humdrum being (Jack) to cease his own self-wringing (to use a word from *Spelt from Sibyl's Leaves*) and wait for God's 'smile' which is 'not wrung'. Apart from the rather tortuous grammar, there are two distinctive Hopkinsian features in this poem that call for comment, the distinctive words and the vitalized colloquialism. 'Size' continues the growth idea of 'root-room' since joy will grow whenever and in whatever form God plans, but it also contains some idea of 'taking aim' or 'considering' as in 'sizing up' a situation or an opponent. 'Betweenpie' constructs a verb out of two elements, the latter one reminding us that in *Pied Beauty* God had fathered forth all that is 'fickle, freckled', and happily conveys the lifegiving and smiling face of the sun suddenly illuminating the 'dapple' of the world. The colloquialisms 'God knows when' and 'God knows what' are potentially understandable in quite opposite senses: in the common usage to indicate that the things referred to are unlikely and incomprehensible, and in Hopkins's literal usage to indicate that God indeed does know exactly when and exactly what. Exasperation and faith are succinctly expressed by the same words.

Hopkins can counter his despair with self-mockery, as he does in *The shepherd's brow*. As in *St. Alphonsus Rodriguez*, he contrasts the heroic with the mundane, but this time with the physical inadequacy rather than the spiritual lack of heroism. Where earlier he bases his views on a faith that God has some purpose, here he laughs himself out of anguish by seeing how easily things become distorted. His own tempests of self-hatred and consciousness of man's fallen state are seen, as we find implied by the spoons and the tempest, as merely a storm in a teacup, his own fire and fever fussy rather than heroic. His consciousness of man's littleness calms the violence of his anger.

There are three other ways in which Hopkins chooses to combat his despair: by imaginative transformation, by prayer and by poetry, though all of these have been implicit in his other poems, poetry in particular helping to knot together the 'strands of man' in him. *That Nature is a Heraclitean Fire and of the Comfort of the Resurrection* is the product of a poet at the height of his powers, and encapsulates large areas with which we are familiar from other places in his writing. It is a poem which mixes the positive and negative elements fully, moving from delighted observation of clouds and their movement, through a recognition of the drying process of the wind and its turning to dust of all man's traces, to a confrontation of the total annihilation of self or individuality. We have been here in *Spelt from Sibyl's Leaves* where we find 'self in self steeped and pashed', and in *The Leaden Echo and the Golden Echo*, where the remedy is similar in that the Resurrection will provide the comfort. Hopkins admits the triviality of the physical world which disturbed him in *The shepherd's brow*:

> Flesh fade, and mortal trash
> Fall to the residuary worm; ' world's wildfire, leave but ash:

but the end of the poem can still be that sense of joy so exuberant that it hurls everything off of the earth except the central core of quality. The joy created by seeing the light in stanza 29 of *The Wreck of the Deutschland*, that had been hymned in *Hurrahing in Harvest*, now is created out of the very depths of his own despairs. The images from his other poems crowd in, his faith asserts his triumph, and even the verse form is part of the argument. The conventional sonnet ends after fourteen lines, at which point in Hopkins's poem man is blotted out by death; but Hopkins probes through layers of appearance to reach significance and refuses to end the sonnet there. Beyond the conventional end he finds the Resurrection, the corruption of the flesh, and then the transformation which he so much desired:

> Manshape, that shone
> Sheer off, disseveral, a star, ' death blots black out; nor mark
>   Is any of him at all so stark
> But vastness blurs and time ' beats level. Enough! the Resurrection,
> A heart's-clarion! Away grief's gasping, ' joyless days, dejection.
>   Across my foundering deck shone
> A beacon, an eternal beam. ' Flesh fade, and mortal trash
> Fall to the residuary worm; ' world's wildfire, leave but ash:

In a flash, at a trumpet crash,
I am all at once what Christ is, ' since he was what I am, and
This Jack, joke, poor potsherd, ' patch, matchwood, immortal diamond,
    Is immortal diamond.

The heroism and promise of this final breakthrough sustained Hopkins through his most arid patches.

Prayer for rain to make fruitful his own private waste land is part of *Thou art indeed just, Lord*, which mixes faith and anger and frustration in a markedly less mannered style. Although he had argued that his style must be distinctive, he also argues (*Letters*, p. 291) that an audience would make his poetry 'more intelligible, smoother, and less singular'. This poem has other reasons than hope of an audience for its being clearer, although his poetry on the whole was becoming more terse, the most significant reason being that it is a translation in its opening lines. From the beginning, then, the reader is aware of the paradox of Hopkins's complaint to God being expressed in the words of Jeremiah (Jeremiah xii.1), with images from the same chapter, and with a consciousness of the answer. Similarly, the strength of the objection is continually softened by the reverent address which punctuates the lines and suspends the force of the sentence and the rhythm:

Thou art indeed just, Lord, if I contend
With thee; but, sir, so what I plead is just.
Why do sinners' ways prosper? and why must
Disappointment all I endeavour end?

Wert thou my enemy, O thou my friend,
How wouldst thou worse, I wonder, than thou dost
Defeat, thwart me? Oh, the sots and thralls of lust
Do in spare hours more thrive than I that spend,

Sir, life upon thy cause.

The complaint that he must be 'Time's eunuch' must be taken in connection with his remark to Bridges that 'I am a eunuch—but it is for the kingdom of heaven's sake', where he is specifically referring to the production of writing, both prose and poetry.

Poetry is the subject of his final poem combating despair, a poem which derives its being from lack of being, which creates from sterility. This poem, *To R. B.*, makes explicit what is obvious throughout Hopkins's work, that he sees faith and poetry as aspects of the same thing. As at the beginning of *The Wreck of the Deutschland*, inspiration is another image of incarnation, poetry a proof of God; here too the poet works through the paradox of a poem whose meaning is denied by the successful expression of that meaning. Coleridge had, like many other Romantic and post-Romantic poets, written of his poetic aridity, and these lines from his *Dejection: an Ode* show how close Hopkins is to a central Romantic tradition:

> For hope grew round me, like the twining vine,
> And fruits, and foliage, not my own, seemed mine.
> But now afflictions bow me down to earth:
> Nor care I that they rob me of my mirth;
>   But oh! each visitation
> Suspends what nature gave me at my birth,
>   My shaping spirit of Imagination.

Hopkins seems even closer to Coleridge's *Work without Hope*:

> All Nature seems at work. Slugs leave their lair—
> The bees are stirring—birds are on the wing—
> And Winter slumbering in the open air,
> Wears on his smiling face a dream of Spring!
> And I the while, the sole unbusy thing,
> Nor honey make, nor pair, nor build, nor sing.

Like Coleridge, Hopkins pits his creative genius against his consciousness of declining powers and, achieving his characteristic movement in 'The roll, the rise, the carol, the creation', he ends by acknowledging the fundamental inadequacy of the unaided self in a wistful finale:

> My winter world, that scarcely breathes that bliss
> Now, yields you, with some sighs, our explanation.

Robert Bridges, sensitive to the character and intentions of his friend, ended on that note. He probably saw the aptness and the shapeliness of ending with a poem which so neatly fulfilled the expectations of another poem written ten years before *The Wreck of the Deutschland* and called *The Alchemist in the City*:

> My window shows the travelling clouds,
> Leaves spent, new seasons, alter'd sky,
> The making and the melting crowds:
> The whole world passes; I stand by.

> They do not waste their meted hours,
> But men and masters plan and build:
> I see the crowning of their towers,
> And happy promises fulfill'd.
>
> And I—perhaps if my intent
> Could count on prediluvian age,
> The labours I should then have spent
> Might so attain their heritage,
>
> But now before the pot can glow
> With not to be discover'd gold,
> At length the bellows shall not blow,
> The furnace shall at last be cold.

Hopkins ended as he began with a consciousness of a task which seemed impossible; yet he does often achieve the impossible alchemy of beauty and sorrow in his poetry. By his own standards and aims it may have been failure, yet it was a failure that he could understand. Writing to Dixon with a wish that he had been elected to the professorship of Poetry at Oxford, Hopkins offered some consolations:

> Above all Christ our Lord: his career was cut short and, whereas he would have wished to succeed by success—for it is insane to lay yourself out for failure, prudence is the first of the cardinal virtues, and he was the most prudent of men—nevertheless he was doomed to succeed by failure; his plans were baffled, his hopes dashed, and his work was done by being broken off undone. However much he understood all this he found it an intolerable grief to submit to it. He left the example: it is very strengthening, but except in that sense it is not consoling. (*Correspondence*, pp. 137–8)

Hopkins aimed to make his life as much as he could a Christian success. That he succeeded through apparent failure, like Christ his example or the nun his literary creation, might have pleased him, both spiritually and aesthetically, as yet another parallel to those on which he had concentrated his life and his poetry.

Index